MOMS:
A Personal
Journal

Paula Hagen
with Vickie LoPiccolo Jennett

Resource Publications, Inc.
San Jose, California

Library of Congress Cataloging in Publication Data
Hagen, Paula, 1937–
MOMS: a personal journal/Paula Hagen with Vickie LoPiccolo Jennett. — Rev. Ed.
p.   cm.
Includes bibliographical references.
ISBN 0-89390-508-9 (alk. paper)
1. Mothers—Religious life. 2. Mothers—Psychology. 3. Motherhood—Psychological
aspects. 4. Motherhood—Religious aspects—Christianity. 5. Self-actualization
(Psychology)—Religious aspects—Christianity. 6. Self-actualization
(Psychology)—Problems, exercises, etc. I. Jennett, Vickie LoPiccolo, 1955– II. Title.
BV4529.18 .H34 2000
248.8'431—dc21   99-088887

Printed in the United States of America
00 01 02 03 04 | 5 4 3 2 1

Editorial directors: Nick Wagner, Kenneth Guentert
Production manager: Elizabeth J. Asborno
Copy editor: William Peatman

About the Cover: "Patchwork Memories" is a Victorian Memory Quilt design
created by Vera M. Klein © 1990, 1996. Each person who stitches the
Memory Quilt personalizes it to express her own memories and individual life
circumstances; the various motifs commemorate significant people and events
in the stitcher's life. Vera graciously agreed to have this needle art appear on the
Personal Journal cover. For more information about this design or for a catalog
of all Vera's cross-stitch designs, please send two first-class stamps along with
your address to: Vera K Designs, 7112 Pan American Freeway, Suite 62,
Albuquerque, NM 87109. Vera's Fax is (505) 856-5189, her phone is
(505) 857-9779, and her e-mail is VeraKxstitch@aol.com.

From Paula

To my Mother and Dad,
who enthusiastically accepted the breath of God at my conception
as a sacred expression of God's love.

To all my sisters and brothers
who shared their toys, held my hand, and walked with me
through dark and scary places.

To the many children—my little friends—
who give me new hope and inspiration
and who deepen my commitment to all God's family.
I've seen the face of God in your spontaneous creativity
and ability to share.

From Vickie

To my entire family—especially Niles—
for patience and support as I continue to spend long hours
writing and creating.

From Both of Us

To all who have nurtured us, trusted us, had faith in us.
Your strength, wisdom and encouragement helped make this journal
and this ministry available to others.

To God—
thanks for being with us and saying:
"Be not afraid, I will show you the way."

Contents

Preface: The Genesis of MOMS

Welcome to *MOMS: A Personal Journal*. Throughout history, countless women have shared the joy and miracle of bringing new life into the world. Those who have taken the time to reflect on their experiences and share their stories have realized more fully the sacredness of their call to motherhood and the challenge of personal spiritual growth.

This journal evolved from more than five years of sharing stories with mothers—hours of laughing, praying, crying and just plain talking with hundreds of women who shared the common bond of motherhood. As time went on, I learned that they also were united by an inner desire—the desire to learn how to live more healthy, complete lives.

As family minister director in a large suburban congregation, I started seeing a pattern among women who came to me looking for someone to lend an ear. Many were surrounded with activities, children, careers, family, and friends, but still they were searching. They felt alone in the frustrations of trying to meet everyone's needs but their own. Some weren't as skilled with friendships as they wanted to be. Others were new to the area due to job relocation or a change in marital status. Most weren't even taking time to think about their own hopes, dreams, and needs. They came seeking someone who would listen. They talked about choices in their lives, about situations that caused anxiety, about feelings of low self-esteem, or about fear. Some discussed fulfilling and successful moments in their lives. Their topics and concerns varied. Yet, woven through each of their stories—even the happy ones—was a feeling of loneliness, of not being connected. They came looking for words of comfort, for an answer. Often the answer these women needed was each other—to talk, to listen, to share their own experiences and wisdom.

They planted the seed and MOMS (Ministry of Mothers Sharing) blossomed and continues to grow. This six-part journal not only respects the importance of each person's role as mother but also recognizes the very personal need to stand back from this tremendous responsibility and simply "be yourself" for a few hours each week. This opportunity to share some basic truths has led to countless friendships that have helped women realize that they aren't alone and that they have many strengths to share with each other.

First we created a simple manual that guided participants through the group experience. MOMS developed into a parish ministry, with outreach to new groups in surrounding areas and then across the country. Soon requests started pouring in from former participants who wanted information they could pass on to their friends. Many women also wanted materials they could refer to when they needed a refresher or to start their own group when they moved to a new area. So, thanks to all those women, you now have in your hands *MOMS: A Personal Journal*. It gathers all the essential features of the ministry and arranges them in journal form so you can use it individually or as part of a MOMS group.

As you continue through this journal, remember that although reflective journal-writing needs to be done alone, many of your thoughts, experiences, and ideas often become more clear and are enriched when shared. Therefore, I encourage you to prayerfully and appropriately share this part of your life journey with others close to you.

Start now to create a short period of personal time in your daily schedule. Establish a place in your home where you can sit down, slow down, and listen to your soul speak to you. As you proceed through this journal, enjoy writing your reflections. If an idea, thought, or problem seems too weighty for you to handle alone or with friends, talk to a counselor or other professional trained to listen. A sense of inner peace is one of the greatest gifts we give ourselves.

Paula Hagen

I was alone. A new mom in a new town. I willingly left a successful career shortly after our first son was born. We moved clear across the country to pursue a professional opportunity for my husband. Life was good. We had each other, our new son, our health, and a wonderful home in the country—yet something was missing. My friends were thousands of miles away. Neighbors brought smiles and covered dishes, but not the intimacy of kindred spirits. I struggled for quite some time trying to understand what I was feeling.

Then, about four years later, the answer come into focus. Not only was I lacking a connectednesss to other women who shared experiences similar to mine, but I also was making the mistake of identifying with the isolated roles in my life rather then concentrating on my "whole self." As a family ministry volunteer, I found many other women who felt competent as a "professional" or as a "mother" or as a "friend" but who, like me, needed to concentrate more on the entire picture—their true selves. Each of us got the support, companionship, and spiritual boost we needed when we came together as the first MOMS group. Our backgrounds, ideas, and interests ran the gamut. Yet our basic values were rooted in God. Still today, we gather for coffee and gut-level talk about our lives and loves.

Had MOMS been around eighteen years ago, I know it would have touched my heart and those in my life. I am thankful that it is here today—not only in group form but especially in book form—so that mothers everywhere can benefit from the wisdom the program offers.

Vickie LoPiccolo Jennett

Acknowledgments

Grateful acknowledgment is extended to all mothers who suggested changes in this updated *Journal* and to Eunice M. Cheshire, Dallas regional MOMS coordinator, and Anne H. And Robert E. Funkhouser Jr., parish family ministry coordinators, who made substantial contributions to the revision.

Grateful acknowledgment is also extended to those granting permission to reprint the following:

"Stress Management Survey," found in Session 2, is printed with permission from Good Apple, Box 299, Carthage, IL 62321, and taken from the book *Living with Stress: Grades 5–9+* (GA1313).

Excerpts from "Little Gidding" in *Four Quartets*, copyright 1943 by T. S. Eliot and renewed in 1971 by Esme Valerie Eliot, reprinted by permission of Harcourt Brace Jovanovich, Inc.

Definition of "grace" from *Webster's New World Dictionary* (3rd College Ed.) © 1988. Used by permission of the publisher, New World Dictionaries/A division of Simon & Schuster, New York.

Introduction

Beginning the Journey

Congratulations for taking time in your busy life to begin this journey. It is an opportunity to reflect on and respond to your spiritual journey. The space we have created on these pages is designed to help you discover in a renewing way the wonder of your own conception—your development as a tiny self who had nine months of growth inside your mother's womb. Soon, the world was yours to discover. In each new discovery, you began to express yourself to those around you. That very self is a divine mystery that will continue to reveal itself to you and to those you love.

Being a mother is a deep commitment of both time and energy. It is one of the roles many of us assume at some point in our lives. All mothers provide a space in their hearts for a growing little person or persons. As mothers, women spend many hours continuing to create safe, nurturing spaces where children can grow and learn. Now, there's a special space just for you—a place where you can get to better know the sacred self that enlivens you, all that you are, and all that you desire to be.

Give yourself the gift of time to enjoy this journal. Set aside time for quiet prayer and reflection. Share with your friends thoughts and experiences that will help you better understand each other and your common ministries of motherhood. Consider sharing your discoveries with your spouse or other family members who are important to you. Recognize that as you take this time to examine your role as a mother, it is important to integrate this with your roles as daughter, friend, wife, etc. Before moving through this journal, think about how you came to be the person you are today.

1. My first memory of life is when _____

_____

_____

_____

_____

2. My first realization that I was special, a unique individual, came when

_____

_____

_____

_____

_____

3. The aspect of myself that I like most right now is _____

_____

_____

_____

_____

_____

4. The talents and qualities I have been given that I relish the most are

_____

_____

_____

_____

_____

5. The individual(s) whom I consider my role model(s) for being a mother/grandmother are: _____

_____

_____

_____

_____

_____

6. The thing that motivates me to take time to do this journal is _____

_____

_____

_____

_____

_____

Notes
And Reflections...

Session 1

Self-Esteem and Self-Acceptance

This section will allow you to:

- **Better understand the meaning of self-esteem.**

- **Be more aware of what influences your self-esteem at this time in your life.**

- **Work through a process that helps you understand why self-acceptance is so important.**

- **Look at images of God's grace for the Christian mother.**

I have called you by name;
you are mine.
— Isaiah 43:1

Prayer Reflection

Throughout this journal, each session begins with a prayer designed to help you focus your attention on your inner self and on the session's subject. As you begin exploring the subject of self-esteem, we ask that you remember these words:

> Do not wish to be anything but what you are, and try to be that perfectly.[1]

"Perfect." Does this word send up a red flag in your mind? When we were children, it meant setting the table in a precise way or tying that absolutely meticulous bow on a birthday present. When we view perfection now as external demands to meet high expectations, it becomes one of life's impossibilities. It can eat away at our very being and can destroy self-esteem. However, when perfection is seen in light of the realization that each of us is a perfect creation, we can begin to accept ourselves just as we are.

In what ways have you accepted yourself "just the way you are"?_____

_____

_____

In what ways are you trying to be more accepting of yourself as God

created you?_____

_____

_____

Keep this in mind as you slowly read and reflect on this psalm from *Psalms of a Laywoman* by Edwina Gateley, VMM:

Called to Become

You are called to become
A perfect creation.
No one is called to become
Who you are called to be.
It does not matter
How short or tall
Or thick-set or slow
You may be.
It does not matter
Whether you sparkle with life
Or are silent as a still pool,
Whether you sing your song aloud
Or weep alone in darkness.
It does not matter
Whether you feel loved and admired
Or unloved and alone.
For you are called to become
A perfect creation.
No one's shadow
Should cloud your becoming,
No one's light
Should dispel your spark.

For the Lord delights in you,
Jealously looks upon you,
And encourages with gentle joy
Every movement of the Spirit
Within you.
Unique and loved you stand,
Beautiful or stunted in your growth
But never without hope and life.
For you are called to become
A perfect creation.
This becoming may be
Gentle or harsh,
Subtle or violent,
But it never ceases.
Never pauses or hesitates,
Only is—
Creative force—
Calling you
Calling you to become
A perfect creation.[2]

My thoughts and feelings about this psalm are _____

_____

_____

_____

One verse that attracted my attention was _____

_____

_____

Understanding Self-Esteem

We can hardly turn on TV or pick up a magazine without being bombarded by images of a "Supermom" who has it all, knows it all, does it all, and still has time for herself. Reality, we know, paints a different picture. When there are deadlines at work, dead fish in the aquarium, an uncooperative washing machine, and kids who need our undivided attention, we aren't sure which role to play. It's tough not to feel as if we have to take personal responsibility for meeting all these demands. Quite frequently we feel threatened by them. In the midst of all this, we need to call a personal Time Out to focus clearly on who we are, so we can do our best to meet the challenges we face each day.

First, it's important to understand where the "self" in self-esteem originates. This ever-changing, ever-growing self has its beginning when God breathes life into a new being. This is the miracle of the conception of the self or human spirit. It is a sacred moment in each of our lives. At that moment, the full potential of each individual is a mystery—a mystery that is revealed gradually over the course of a lifetime.

Each person is unique because of the parental combination (genetic sperm and ovum), the environment, and the infusion of God's love. Therefore, each person (self) is born unique, sacred, and precious. Once a child is born into this world, parents and others in the child's environment help that person develop a sense of self-esteem.

From our conception and for all eternity, God loves each of us totally and unconditionally just as we are. Our acceptance of this reality provides us with a solid foundation on which strong self-esteem is formed. We suggest that there are four inter-related aspects that influence our self-esteem. Let's take a moment to reflect on these four areas.

Self-Awareness — I am sacred; each of us is sacred.

I am becoming aware of my "true self" when I _____

_____

_____

_____

Self-Respect — I respect myself and my needs.

I respect my needs when I_____

_____

_____

Self-Worth — I am special and have value.

I like myself when I_____

_____

_____

Self-Confidence — I can develop skills of self-expression and self-care.

I am learning to take care of myself by _____

_____

_____

I am able to express myself when I _____

_____

_____

_____

Looking back on our childhood years can help us better understand these four components of self-esteem. Although the development of self-esteem is quite complex, for discussion purposes here we will simplify the concept. Let's view self-esteem as being passed on from one generation to the next. Our parents and others in our environment made choices about how they would grow in self-awareness, self-respect, self-worth, and self-confidence. Their choices were based on their life experiences, as were their parents' choices before them. Ideally, our parents tried to guide each of us to make good choices that would develop a healthy sense of self-esteem. However, in some instances, parents are not able to make healthy choices for themselves, so their behaviors and words may not create the model nurturing environment for their families. We need to remember that this doesn't create an insurmountable roadblock in the pathway to healthy self-esteem, although it may feel that way at times. Rather than idealizing parenthood, we need to be realistic about the past and move forward, learning to make small decisions and choices that begin to answer our own needs.

Typically, as we grow, we become more independent. The choices we make—although sometimes influenced by those around us—become our own. Today, as mothers, we are inundated with opportunities to make choices. There are the simple, day-to-day choices like selecting a color for the new carpet or deciding what to wear. We make scores of those choices every day—we could do it in our sleep. We also make some more weighty choices—the ones that influence our self-awareness, self- respect, self-worth, and self-confidence. We need to consider those in relationship with us, both as we make choices and as they do likewise. Mutual respect is especially important throughout the growth process.

Think for a moment about the choices you make.

What choice did you make today that influenced your self-esteem? _____

_____

_____

_____

_____

As we reflect on our past, we become aware of some of the choices we made—or allowed others to make for us—that have neither increased our self-esteem nor enhanced our self-confidence. The examples are many: The time we gave in to pressure from friends and took that piece of candy without paying for it. Or our repeated cowering before a parent who plies us with guilt about something we did or didn't do. Perhaps even harsh responses to our children or spouse when we're really angry about something else.

We know that those around us can influence the choices we make. However, we also need to understand that, ultimately, each of us is responsible for making our own choices. And, as we realize we have the power to make these choices, we become more responsible for our self-esteem. We can't rearrange our past or control others in our environment, but we can become more aware of our choices each day. We can choose to make new responses to life situations. Many women have moved from a feeling of powerlessness over choices (low self-esteem) to a healthy sense of their ability to make choices.

Think back to how you grew in self-awareness and self-confidence. Look at the decision-making process in your daily life and how this impacts your self-esteem. Jot down important choices you have made.

1. _____

_____

_____

_____

2. _____

_____

_____

_____

What effect did they have in your life?

1. _____

_____

2. _____

_____

Many of us are generally comfortable with the choices we make. We try to respond appropriately to everyday stresses. Usually, we say what we think and feel good about our response. Yet, throughout a typical day or week, there are times when we're less sure about a decision we make. Then there are situations in which we feel as if we've lost all control.

Take the example of one twenty-five year old in a MOMS Group who, after two failed marriages and taking sole responsibility for children ages seven and three, was overwhelmed by the fact that her choices continued to lower her self-respect, self-awareness, and self-esteem. She cried out in fear and anger at her therapist and her parents: "They gave me all this money and advice but didn't show me how to make a healthy choice for myself." While discussing her situation with other women in the MOMS Group, she realized: "They didn't know they were making unhealthy choices in their own lives. How could they teach me? Now I've got to learn what choices and decisions are healthy for me."

This realization started her and her children on the path to a drastically changed, more healthy lifestyle. She was able to make a series of choices that gradually led to self-acceptance.

In a few well-chosen words, T.S. Eliot is able to capture the essence of continuing along the path toward true self-acceptance:

> We shall not cease from exploration
> And the end of all our exploring
> Will be to arrive where we started
> And know the place for the first time.[3]

The Pathway Toward Accepting Yourself

As we grow in self-esteem and examine the components of this dimension of ourselves, we become aware of a continuing process or pathway that ultimately leads to a genuine sense of self-acceptance. Diagram 1 illustrates the steps we take on this pathway. Like traveling along any path, we may move forward or slide back in the process of consciously striving to develop and maintain a healthy sense of self-acceptance.

> After looking at Diagram 1, think about your movement along the pathway toward self-acceptance. Where on the pathway do you find yourself right now? Remember that this is a cyclic process that each individual repeats again and again throughout life. Although the steps are numbered, there is no value associated with being "higher" or "lower.

I am at step_____

> How do you feel about where you are on the pathway?

I feel_____

_____

_____

Would I like to be at a different step on the pathway? _____

_____

_____

_____

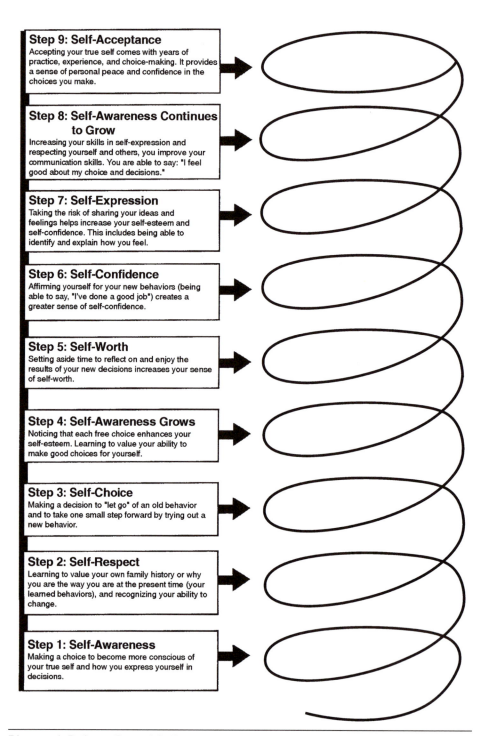

Step 9: Self-Acceptance
Accepting your true self comes with years of practice, experience, and choice-making. It provides a sense of personal peace and confidence in the choices you make.

Step 8: Self-Awareness Continues to Grow
Increasing your skills in self-expression and respecting yourself and others, you improve your communication skills. You are able to say: "I feel good about my choice and decisions."

Step 7: Self-Expression
Taking the risk of sharing your ideas and feelings helps increase your self-esteem and self-confidence. This includes being able to identify and explain how you feel.

Step 6: Self-Confidence
Affirming yourself for your new behaviors (being able to say, "I've done a good job") creates a greater sense of self-confidence.

Step 5: Self-Worth
Setting aside time to reflect on and enjoy the results of your new decisions increases your sense of self-worth.

Step 4: Self-Awareness Grows
Noticing that each free choice enhances your self-esteem. Learning to value your ability to make good choices for yourself.

Step 3: Self-Choice
Making a decision to "let go" of an old behavior and to take one small step forward by trying out a new behavior.

Step 2: Self-Respect
Learning to value your own family history or why you are the way you are at the present time (your learned behaviors), and recognizing your ability to change.

Step 1: Self-Awareness
Making a choice to become more conscious of your true self and how you express yourself in decisions.

Diagram 1: Pathway Toward Self-Acceptance (see explanation, page 13)

God's Grace: Source of All Human Life

Quite often we take for granted the energy that fuels our soul, our very being. We acknowledge God as the creator of the universe and source of all energy and life, yet we spend only small amounts of time actually reflecting on this gift. Taking time to explore the origins of our very being, our true self, really can have a practical impact on the way we face each day. This type of reflection can help us live life more fully by guiding us to use our God-given ability to make healthy choices.

To help you with a basic understanding of grace, we've included part of the definition from Webster's *New World Dictionary*:

> ...a special virtue, gift or help given to a person by God.[4]

Taking this one step further, in her book *Transforming Grace: Christian Tradition and Woman's Experience,* noted theologian Anne E. Carr brings the individual recipient of grace into the picture:

> Grace is the gift of claiming responsibility for one's life as love of self as well as love of others, as the assumption of healthy power over one's life and circumstances.[5]

The challenge to us as women is to keep our love of self balanced with our love of others as we use this God-given ability to make healthy choices for ourselves and with those we love. Each of us experiences the dynamic interplay of God's grace or energy in our thoughts, our feelings and our intuitions as we try to make decisions.

How do you feel about the balance between your love of self and your love of others?

I feel _____

_____

_____

_____

What kind of grace, wisdom, strength or help are you praying for today?

I am praying for _____

_____

_____

_____

Each individual is influenced by parents, family, friends and others in the environment. Simply put, those who receive affirmation and nurturing are more likely to develop a healthy self-esteem and be able to accept themselves. Those who are criticized and rejected throughout life often feel inadequate, are unable to cope, and struggle with acceptance of their true selves.

Most of us experience a combination of both positive and negative responses to our decisions and choices in our formative years and throughout our lives. Now, as adults, even when our sense of self-esteem dips to an all-time low, we are able to choose to get back in touch with our true self and with God's grace. At any point in life, the unique person that is "me" can choose to reclaim the sacredness of life in a new way; to take the first step toward attaining a new balance between the love of self and the love of others; and to make healthier choices that have positive impacts on our self-esteem.

Because any growth in self-awareness may be filled with emotion, it helps to share this new awareness with a person you trust and know well. The perceptions of a close friend are valuable during the growth process. Remember, you need not grow alone.

Also important are quiet time and reflection, which help us to integrate our thoughts, feelings and intuitions into a healthy decision-making process. Frequently, we turn to God in prayer for the grace, energy, wisdom or strength to be able to express our true selves and to allow others to do the same. Keep this in mind as you enjoy writing out your own ideas and feelings on the next page.

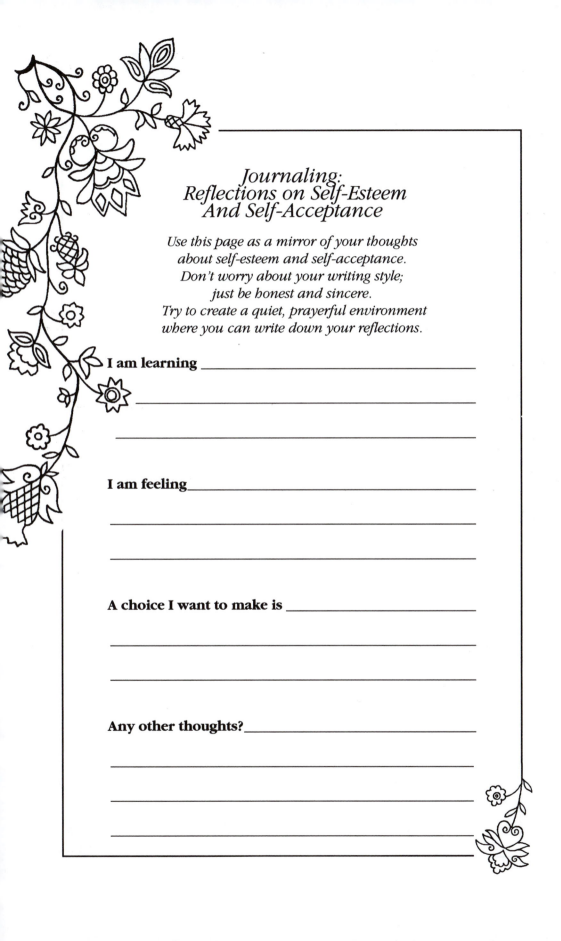

Journaling:
Reflections on Self-Esteem And Self-Acceptance

*Use this page as a mirror of your thoughts
about self-esteem and self-acceptance.
Don't worry about your writing style;
just be honest and sincere.
Try to create a quiet, prayerful environment
where you can write down your reflections.*

I am learning _____

_____

_____

I am feeling _____

_____

_____

A choice I want to make is _____

_____

_____

Any other thoughts? _____

_____

_____

_____

*More Notes
And Reflections...*

Session 2

Stress, Worries, and Anxiety

This section will provide an opportunity for you to:

- **Engage in honest communication**
about your stress as the mother of a family.

- **Look at the relationship**
between the highest areas of stress in your life
and your values, attitudes, and needs.

- **Consider ways to be true to your self**
and to reduce stress by taking care of your true self.

- **Examine healthy ways to deal with stress, worries, and anxieties.**

"Come to me, you who work hard and carry heavy burdens.
I will give you rest."
— Matthew 11:28

Prayer Reflection

Take a few minutes to quiet yourself—both body and mind. (Sometimes lighting a candle serves to focus our attention on our inner light and strength.) Read this passage slowly and thoughtfully.

> For this reason,
> I bow my knees before God
> who is Mother and Father to us all.
> From whom every family
> in heaven and on earth is named.
> That according to the riches
> of God's glory,
> you may be granted strength, with might
> through the Spirit
> in your inmost being,
> and that Christ may dwell
> in your hearts through faith;
> that you, being rooted and grounded in love,
> may have power to comprehend with all the Saints
> what is the breadth and length and height and depth,
> and to know the love of Christ,
> which surpasses knowledge,
> that you may be filled with all the fullness of God.
>
> Now to the One who by the power
> at work within us is able to do far more abundantly
> than all that we ask or think,
> to God be glory in the Church and in Christ Jesus
> to all generations,
> for ever and ever, Amen.
> — Ephesians 3:14–21[6]

What phrase especially attracted your attention as you read these words?

_____

_____

Redefining Stress: Worry and Anxiety

As parents, we are in the unique position of watching our children grow, while at the same time, growing with them ourselves.

We delight in watching our children. We experience pleasure and joy as we see our child's "true self" emerge, as each child learns to "do it myself." This pride and sense of satisfaction begins with a child's first word, first step, or new experiences, ideas, or feelings. We continue to marvel as children grow, change, and master that algebra concept or land that all-important job. As mothers, we spontaneously lend a helping hand or heart by encouraging and supporting our children. The maternal sense that a child is learning a unique way to express his or her true self is something that's just there—a sort of sixth sense. We give children the courage to try new things and the permission to be imperfect as they grow and learn new skills.

We need to give ourselves the same permission.

Just as growing up is a series of new tasks and experiences, motherhood is a growth process that centers around the mystery of sharing one's self while nurturing and nourishing life within the whole family system. Ask most mothers and they would agree that it helps to have a friend—someone with whom to share words of wisdom and encouragement, someone who gives them the freedom to be imperfect as they work through the stress, worry, and anxiety of the new tasks and situations that accompany motherhood. Formal training and continuing education are required for many professions, but not for motherhood. In many instances, training takes place the hard way—through trial and error. Often the true wisdom comes only after many years. "If I knew grandchildren were so much fun," the saying goes, "I would have had them first." This process of "growing as we learn" is part of God's plan. The task is to live our lives with personal integrity and self-responsibility.

As we progress through the challenges of motherhood (and, actually, any phase in our lives), we become aware of stress much the way we do of automotive trouble when the warning gauges on our dashboards light up. Small signals alert us to the fact that something is amiss. Our backs ache. We react with a scream. We get tired. We're easily frustrated. When these red lights come on, we need to look at some of the choices available.

- Slow down and take a look before permanent damage is done.

- "Let go" of an old behavior or attitude that causes stress to increase.

- Take better care of ourselves and express our true self.

- Put up some boundaries that help us deal with the causes of stress that are outside ourselves. (Set limits, learn to say "no.")

- Look at diet and exercise levels in our lives. Consider a change, if needed.

- Do something—speak out—about the causes of stress.

Because each of us is unique, our stress levels cannot be compared. What creates turmoil for one may be routine for another. This is because all people feel and express their values in a unique way. Stress is the conflict between our values, needs, and expectations. Tension also can result from the behaviors we choose to use to fulfill our values, needs, or expectations. Many times as we clarify our needs and expectations, we are able to better understand what we really value and what is causing the stress. In order to lower stress, it helps to choose some new behaviors.

Consider the example of the mother who was surprised that her friend was at wit's end when raising one toddler and two teens. "But, it's got to be easy having the older kids to help out," commented the mother, whose children were ages three and seven.

"Well, having the extra hands can sometimes be a help," the friend said, "but you have no idea what it's like to go from having two relatively independent children to suddenly having a little one again. And, you can't imagine the balancing act of trying to deal with the hormones of a teenage girl, the whims of a junior-high boy, and the demands of a little one. The house is a mess and I just don't have any time for myself." This woman valued making time for self, making time for the kids, and having a clean house. She expected to do all of these things in exemplary fashion. She needed some time for herself so she could better understand how to lower expectations and feel good about all that was going on in her life.

Both women in the previous example agree that it's possible to adopt behaviors that help them put stress in the proper perspective. Here are some "guidelines" about stress reduction that were developed by mothers participating in a stress-reduction seminar.

Guideline 1 — Define your highest stress issue(s) or time(s). Look at what is draining your energy; bring whatever it is to a conscious level. Ask yourself what is causing the anxious mind, the negative feelings, and the tense body. Write it down. Talk it out. Go for a walk. Do whatever you need to get it in perspective. Remember that stress is a normal part of life. Learning to deal with it is an essential skill that lasts a lifetime.

Two areas of stress in my life right now are:

1. _____

2. _____

I think I know what causes the stress:

1. _____

2. _____

When I experience this stress, I feel: _____

_____

_____

My usual way of coping is: _____

_____

When we come to view stress as a part of life that we can deal with rather than something we try to get rid of, we are able to put it in the proper perspective.

Guideline 2 — Begin to set clear limits or boundaries; protect yourself from unnecessary stress. Then take time to create an alternate response to the situation(s) that create stress for you. Only you can learn to say "no" to outside stress so that you can say "yes" to the things you value and need. Setting the boundary allows you the time you need to be true to yourself and to be creative in your response to the situation. Some everyday examples of setting limits are:

- *Establishing a budget.* Many months, balancing the checkbook is a painful exercise of making limited dollars cover what seem to be unlimited expenses. So often we say we're going to set a budget, or we have a vague idea of spending limits in our heads. But rarely do we find and take the time to sit down and look carefully at balancing income and things we really need. Make a "wish list" of things not in the regular budget and consider buying them as extra funds become available. Budgeting provides concrete knowledge that can help calm the stress that comes from worrying about not having a clear picture of finances.

- *Creating low-stress ways to remind young children of time limits.* Dinnertime, bedtime, and the end of playtime create havoc around most homes with toddlers. After being repeated three or four times, a well-intentioned "let's clean up" often becomes a frustrated command. Use the timer on your stove or invest in an egg timer. Give the kids advance warning that in a few minutes the bell will ring and it's time to get to bed or move on to the next task. Frequently a change as simple as this can save tired vocal chords and, more importantly, strained nerves.

Frequent fatigue is one symptom or warning sign that helps alert mothers that they've been giving too much without taking or replenishing their energy supply. As energy sources wane, mothers often feel like the depleted balance of an overextended budget or crowded pages on an overbooked activity calendar. Unless a change is made, a crisis looms ahead. A common response experienced in these situations is guilt—guilt because of what isn't being done, guilt because of fatigue. However, when mothers become aware that their "personal energy sheet" is out of balance, they are able to turn guilty feelings into constructive measures for rebalancing their energy levels. *Remember, it's not your responsibility to ensure that family members and friends are always happy and content. It's OK to say, "No!" to requests that tax your resources.*

Personal energy includes all aspects of a person's life—physical, emotional, and spiritual. The amount of personal and psychic energy required varies for each lifestyle—as does each person's ability to meet the energy requirements. Only you can become aware of or already know your expectations and limitations, so only you can set healthy boundaries on how much time, money, and energy you pour out. Although it isn't healthy to compare your energy level to that of other women, it does help to talk things over with others in similar situations and to learn how they select to meet the demands placed on their energy. Generally, mothers tend to be hard on themselves and not provide enough personal time—when really, this is what they need to refuel and reenergize.

One to three things I do for my own personal renewal are:

1. _____

2. _____

3. _____

Guideline 3 — Build yourself a healthy and trustworthy group of women with whom you can be honest and candid about your stress level. Choose those with similar values and a positive attitude about their ability to learn conflict resolution skills, assertiveness, and decision-making skills. Remember that gossip, moaning, and chattering about resentments drain psychic energy. Work to rid yourself of those behaviors. If you need help beyond that of friends, seek out a professional. (Call your physician to get a referral.) One session with a skilled professional may cure months of high anxiety, stress, and worry. Remember, new behaviors can be learned!

1. Name a few friends who make up (or could make up) this group.

_____

_____

_____

2. Name a few places where you might find a friend_____

_____

_____

3. List the steps you will need to take to establish this friendship support

group_____

_____

_____

_____

_____

_____

Guideline 4 — Continue to develop communication skills with friends who can help you set and maintain healthy expectations and boundaries on your energy output. Save some of your spirit and energy just for yourself. Allow yourself time to think, feel, create, and choose.

To help you work through your feelings about stress, we have included a survey that allows you to identify stress-inducing areas in your life. It is one of the activities for personal growth included in *Living With Stress*, a book designed especially for young students.[7] However, its comprehensive nature and understandable approach make it an ideal tool for all ages. It is encouraging to see that many schools today are teaching children to identify what is causing them stress so that parents and teachers can help them make some new choices and learn some new skills before problems reach a crisis level. Completing this survey will provide you with a general picture of where you might want to start making some new choices.

For further insight, take a look at Dolores Curran's *Stress and the Healthy Family*. You'll realize you're not alone! Her twelve conclusions on family stress were developed following much research and many interviews with families. Most parents find her ideas practical and useful.8

Once you've answered all the questions, tabulate your scores and look at the category where you find your lowest scores. Remember that this is a general tool designed for a variety of lifestyles. Go back and reread the statements that you marked low. A low score doesn't necessarily signal the existence of stress in your life or that a change is needed. It may just be a situation that has little or no application to you. On the other hand, it may be the key to a change you need to make. Be honest in your assessment. Do your low scores represent values that really are a part of your true self but ones that you have been neglecting? If so, they may be contributing to stress in your life. Remember that managing stress is a basic tool that can help all members of your family maintain a healthy balance in your lives.

Consider using this tool with your family. Once everyone has completed it, discuss ways in which each person can help lower personal and family stress.

Stress Management Survey

The following questionnaire is designed to help you assess where you think you are at this time regarding your ability to manage stress.

Put the number in each box that best indicates your response according to the following scale:

4 = Usually; 3 = Often; 2 = Sometimes; 1 = Seldom; 0 = Never

After you have responded to all of the questions, add your score for each section. Transfer these scores to the appropriate box on the pie graph at the end.

Personal Development

	Usually	Often	Sometimes	Seldom	Never
1. I believe I am in control of my life.					
2. I enjoy being alone for some time during the day.					
3. I am at peace with myself.					
4. I can laugh easily.					
5. I can identify and solve the problems in my life.					
6. I am aware of outside forces that affect my feelings.					
7. I like myself.					
8. I have an ongoing plan for personal growth.					
Total					

Interpersonal Development

	Usually	Often	Sometimes	Seldom	Never
1. I can easily think of five people with whom I can play.					
2. I can relate well to people in my family.					
3. I am a good listener.					
4. I am a good friend.					
5. When I have a difficult problem, it is easy for me to ask for help.					
6. I let my friends and family know that I appreciate them.					
7. I enjoy communicating and am interested in what others have to say.					
8. When I am aware of them, I admit my mistakes to others.					
Total					

Physical Development

	Usually	Often	Sometimes	Seldom	Never
1. I pay attention to the quantity and quality of the foods I eat.					
2. I enjoy stretching, moving, and exerting my body.					
3. I choose low-fat foods in restaurants.					
4. I do at least one form of vigorous physical exercise several times a week.					
5. I have a good appetite and weigh within ten pounds of my ideal weight.					
6. I have regular bowel movements.					
7. I eat at least two raw fruits every day.					
8. I eat at least two servings of vegetables every day.					
Total					

Intellectual Development

	Usually	Often	Sometimes	Seldom	Never
1. It is easy for me to concentrate for thirty minutes at a time.					
2. I can temporarily set aside a problem and enjoy myself.					
3. I use positive thoughts and beliefs to make things happen the way I would like them to.					
4. I believe that no problem is too big to solve.					
5. I learn at least one new thing every day.					
6. I enjoy new experience.					
7. I actively explore my natural surroundings.					
8. I treat what I do not know how to do as a challenge and eventually learn how to do it.					
Total					

Values Development

	Usually	Often	Sometimes	Seldom	Never
1. I can accept knowing things without knowing how I know them.					
2. I believe that I am an integral part of a greater reality.					
3. I experience a sense of wonder and awe when I contemplate the universe.					
4. When I am ill, I play an active role in speeding up my healing process.					
5. I pay attention to my dreams.					
6. I allow others to have beliefs different than my own.					
7. It is acceptable with me if some things are unknowable to my mind.					
8. I look at problems as opportunities for growth.					
Total					

Time Management

	Usually	Often	Sometimes	Seldom	Never
1. I set daily goals.					
2. I have a long-range plan of action for something I want to accomplish.					
3. I assign priorities to the things I have to do.					
4. I am able to list my priorities and do the important things first.					
5. I am on time.					
6. I am in control of my day.					
7. My day goes smoothly.					
8. I set goals that are attainable.					
Total					

Stress Management Scale

1. Add the total number of points for each section of the Stress Management Survey.

2. Put the total for each section in the box near the section name on the graph below.

3. Indicate these total on the pie graph. Darken the area from the center of the graph to your score.

This graph gives you a visual picture of those areas in your life where you manage stress very well, as well as those areas in your life that need improvement.

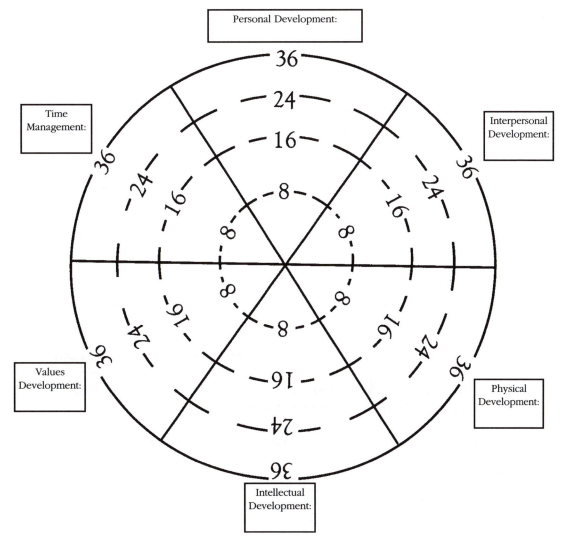

Seeing How God's Grace Helps Us Handle Stress

God's grace is a special energy that comes with the practice of faith or belief in a Higher Power, Supreme Being, or God. For Christians, the two phrases Jesus spoke most often—"Be not afraid" and "Peace be with you"—are words of wisdom firmly planted in the mind. How do we move those words of wisdom from our minds into our hearts? How do we infuse those simple but meaningful ideas into our choices and our intuition about the future? We can do this by realizing that life is a series of events that awaken us to God's presence in our world and in our daily tasks. In this fast-paced, high-technology, and sometimes violent world, being peaceful and dealing with stress in a healthy way requires that a conscious choice be made. In order to make that choice, we need to establish some concrete behaviors:

- Take time each day to get in touch with God in your innermost being. A daily prayer, short meditation, scripture reading, or time of silence before a lit candle helps us focus on God's energy within us and on our own inner wisdom. Even five or ten minutes in the morning before others rise can be helpful.

- Set aside a regular, short but consistent time of physical exercise—some sort of body work that you find enjoyable— to release the tension and anxiety stored in the body. This can be done alone, with someone else, or in a group. The important thing isn't what you do but that you do it.

- Make it a point to spend some regular communication time with adult friends who share your values and concerns. Don't become isolated.

- Begin recording your thoughts and feelings on paper. Writing down ideas and experiences, then thinking about and discussing them is an excellent way to open the conscious mind to your innermost feelings—feelings that contain wisdom and energy.

Before continuing, make a resolution to take one small step to try to reduce stress in your life.

The stress is _____

_____

_____

_____

I resolve to deal with this stress by_____

_____

_____

_____

I will try to reduce it by _____

_____

_____

_____

As you begin or continue to make time each day for prayer or medita-tion, remember that the essence of Christian prayer is slowing down to respond to God, to inner wisdom, to the eternal light, to the unconditional love that lies deep within each person—your innermost self, spirit or soul. Simply being aware of a desire to pray is a prayer in itself. These words of the Desert Fathers and Mothers of the third century ring true today: "If you want to pray, you are already praying."[9]

One MOMS group compiled this collage of thoughts from letters St. Paul wrote to his fellow Christians nearly two thousand years ago. The women were surprised to find that still today we're working to apply these princi-ples to our lives:

Your strength comes from God's mighty power within you...
In everything you do, stay away from complaining...
Tell God your needs and don't forget to thank God
   for all blessings.
Fix your thoughts on what is true and good and right.
Think about things that are pure and lovely...
And dwell on the fine, good things in others.
Don't spend your time worrying about things...
Be gentle and be ready to forgive; never hold grudges.
Most of all, let love guide your life...
Let the peace of heart which comes from Christ be always present
in your hearts and lives for this is your responsibility
   and privilege (TLB).[10]

This ancient wisdom applies to my life in this way: _____

_____

_____

_____

To me, "peace of heart" is _____

_____

_____

The "peace of heart" I desire is _____

_____

_____

_____

While keeping this "peace of heart" at the forefront of your thoughts, allow yourself to be at ease and enjoy the images that come to mind. Taking time for reflection is not idle time. It is valuable time for both mental and physical health. Remember, it helps to set aside a regular time and find a quiet, relaxed location where you can write out your ideas and intuitions.

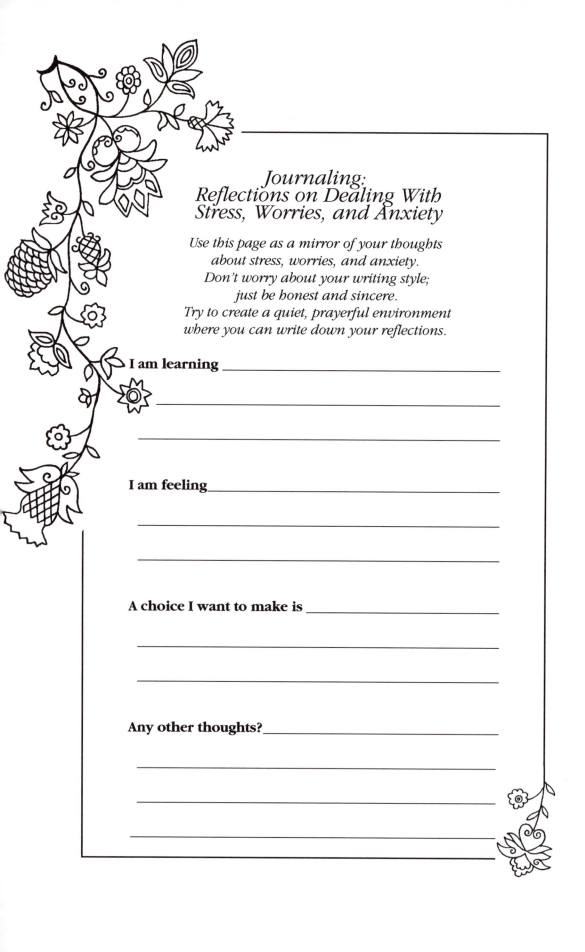

Journaling:
Reflections on Dealing With
Stress, Worries, and Anxiety

Use this page as a mirror of your thoughts
about stress, worries, and anxiety.
Don't worry about your writing style;
just be honest and sincere.
Try to create a quiet, prayerful environment
where you can write down your reflections.

I am learning _____

_____

_____

I am feeling _____

_____

_____

A choice I want to make is _____

_____

_____

Any other thoughts? _____

_____

_____

_____

Session 3

Everyday Spirituality

This section is designed to:

• **Help you begin to articulate your experiences of spirituality and your awareness of God in your life.**

• **Increase your awareness that motherhood has an important impact on your spiritual growth.**

• **Strengthen your sense of motherhood as a special and unique call to wholeness, holiness, and ministry.**

I will praise the God of our Lord Jesus Christ
who has given me every spiritual blessing in Christ.
— Ephesians 1:3

The Sacred in Daily Life: A Meditation

We look at creation—a spectacular sunset, a spirited child, a blossoming teenager, a wise older person, a beautiful flower—and we see the beauty of God alive and working. But rarely do most of us stop to reflect prayerfully on God's beauty revealed in our own daily life. Yet God is alive—in the flood of mundane tasks and obligations as well as in the milestones of our lives. This is where everyday spirituality comes in. It's the realization that with each choice we make, we are using the power God gave each of us to co-create a whole person, a unique individual. By taking a few minutes each day to focus just on yourself, you will come to realize more fully how God is working in and through you. Here are a few ideas to get you started reflecting on the person that is "me."

In the following meditation, you are invited to look at your whole self—your body, your mind, your commitments, relationships, and personal experiences—all the ways in which you externally express your inner soul through concrete behavior. This is a meditation on areas where you are awakening to the sacred in your everyday life. Ideally it is completed in conjunction with "The Whole Spiritual Person" wheel (Diagram 2). Think about the ways in which your inner-self, soul, and inner-spirituality flow out into your daily physical, social, and emotional activities.

My Sacred Self

Physical — The part of my body that I like the most is_____

_____

Emotional — My favorite feeling is a feeling of_____

_____

Commitments — A commitment that I have made that I relish is _____

_____

_____

Intellectual — The thing I like knowing the most is _____

_____

_____

Relationships — The relationship that is the most precious to me right now

is _____

_____

What aspect of my whole person is the hardest for me to see as sacred?

_____

_____

Your reflective answers are precious and sacred. Listen to your heart as you share them with a friend who can listen and be non-judgmental. Being able to share these reflections is a prayer in itself.

Take time to meditate and share with another person your ideas and feelings. Gradually, you will recognize—and give to those in your life—a greater sense of the sacredness of choices, activities, and events in your life. All facets of living take on a new richness, a richness not tied to material things, when viewed in this light. We continue this sense of sacredness by seeing our energy and health as great blessings that need to be appreciated, nurtured, and developed fully.

The Whole Spiritual Person

Spirituality is not a clear-cut, isolated component of our lives. Rather, spirituality is the core inner connection that ties together all aspects of a human being. It is the way we live and relate to life.

In an attempt to capture the complexity of the human person and the interrelatedness of various aspects of the person, the pie- shaped diagram or wheel is used. This diagram may help you see spirituality in a new way in your life.

In the outer circle of the diagram, we see five areas in which each individual experiences growth and development of the true self. Our spiritual self radiates out into each of these areas. At a very early age, this true self begins to reveal itself in the family. For most, the home is the first place where we learn to share our feelings, commitments, ideas, dreams, and relationships. From our parents and other adults, we learn that we are sacred—that our body is a sacred home for our spirit. We come to see that we are able to have intimate relationships with others and with God.

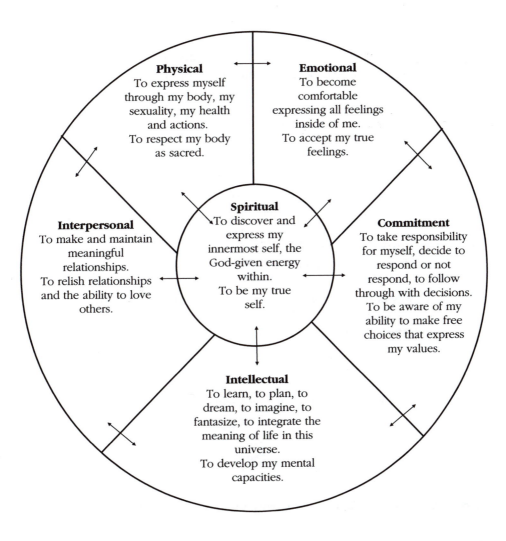

Physical
To express myself through my body, my sexuality, my health and actions.
To respect my body as sacred.

Emotional
To become comfortable expressing all feelings inside of me.
To accept my true feelings.

Spiritual
To discover and express my innermost self, the God-given energy within.
To be my true self.

Interpersonal
To make and maintain meaningful relationships.
To relish relationships and the ability to love others.

Commitment
To take responsibility for myself, decide to respond or not respond, to follow through with decisions.
To be aware of my ability to make free choices that express my values.

Intellectual
To learn, to plan, to dream, to imagine, to fantasize, to integrate the meaning of life in this universe.
To develop my mental capacities.

Diagram 2: Whole Spiritual Person

A Mother's Spirituality

The typical daily conversation rarely centers on spirituality. This is largely because of all the practical, gotta-get-done tasks and topics that flood our agendas. But when we step back and look at our day, we realize that it actually is the mundane tasks and routine rituals that contribute to our spirituality.

Now, let's take a few minutes and think about our spirituality and how it is influenced by our role of mothering. This role influences our relationships and how we use our time. These definitions compiled by other women may be helpful to you as you reflect on your experience.

Spirituality is...

"Seeking a relationship with God...trying to touch the Divine through the simplicity and totality of our experiences."[11]

"One's experience of God in faith and the way one responds concretely to God within a community of believers."[12]

"Our way of being in the world, our way of doing whatever we do in the light of being touched, held, delighted by, and rooted in the Mystery of Divinity ...."[13]

Which definition best describes your experiences? _____

_____

My relationship with God or my spirituality since I've been a mother is one

of_____

_____

_____

Women who are mothers have the unique experience both of being created in the image and likeness of God and of being co-creators of the next generation. Although many authors (some of whom are moms) write about this important and sacred privilege/responsibility, few mothers have the time to write about their own personal spiritual experiences.

When asked to define spirituality, many people hesitate, then say something about organized religion rather than actually putting words to their own image of spirituality. Others look to organized religion or the Church to define spirituality. Yet each of us does have a unique image of spirituality that colors our daily behaviors. Common, everyday spirituality is what gives life meaning. It is as basic as breathing, thinking, walking, talking, and being part of the human race. Take some time now to use your intuition and imagination to sort out the images, colors, and experiences that come to mind when you ponder the word spirituality.

My sense of spirituality is _____

_____

_____

_____

Rather than going to a dictionary or another book to see if your ideas are in line with the "official" definition, share your thoughts, images, and experiences of spirituality with a friend or group of women who are willing to discuss their ideas and experiences as they relate to daily life.

Seeing Motherhood As Ministry

Since the time of Jesus, Christians have struggled with a definition for "ministry." Some see it as a formal commitment to a specific religious role. Others view ministry as helping out or volunteering wherever needed in their community or parish. Still others view ministry as a basic response to the sacredness in each person. However we see it, ministry requires a balance between giving to others and receiving what we need.

A long time ago, Christ's disciple Peter gave us these words that help us understand the balance we need in our lives:

> God has given each of you some special abilities; be sure to use
> them to help each other, passing on to others God's many kinds
> of blessings. — 1 Peter 4:10[14]

As we grow in a sense of our inner goodness and spirituality, we are able to respond to the sacredness in others. In the early Church, Christ's followers were known by the way they loved each other. In Paul's letters to the Corinthians, we see this perspective.

> Blessed be the God ... the God of all consolation, who comforts
> us in all our sorrows, so that we can offer others, in their sorrows,
> the consolation that we have received from God ourselves.
> — 2 Corinthians 1:3–5[15]

Take a few minutes to write out your reflections about how you respond to the needs of others and how you allow others to respond to your needs. Look at your own children, family, co- workers, neighbors, and friends.

In my life, I minister to _____

_____

_____

_____

I do this by _____

_____

_____

_____

These are the people who minister to me: _____

_____

_____

They do this by _____

_____

_____

Women, in their role as mothers, often do many seemingly routine and commonplace tasks without reflecting on these activities as a "service" or as a "gift of self" to another. These are not duties or obligations; rather, they are acts of love and concern that answer daily needs of those around us.

One woman put it this way:

> "As a mom, it's tough to see trips to the dentist, baseball games
> on sweltering days, and drinks of water in the night as ministry.
> But, you know, it really makes me feel like I'm doing something
> special when I look at it in that light. Helping with homework
> becomes a joy and not a chore."

Remember, the ministry of our everyday tasks can be an expression of our inner spirituality. Take a few minutes to look at your life in this light and define "ministry" as it applies to you.

My ministry is _____

_____

_____

_____

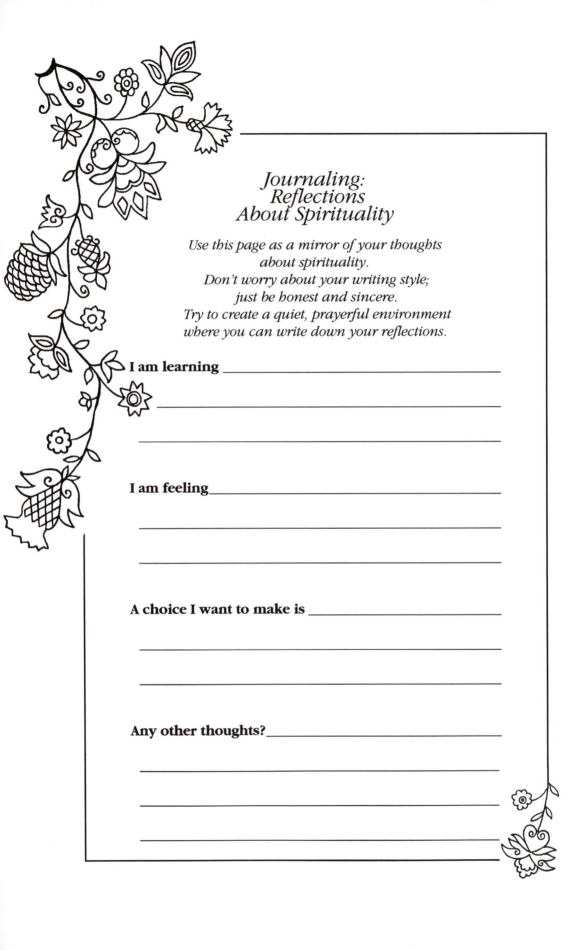

Journaling: Reflections About Spirituality

Use this page as a mirror of your thoughts about spirituality.
Don't worry about your writing style;
just be honest and sincere.
Try to create a quiet, prayerful environment
where you can write down your reflections.

I am learning _____

_____

_____

I am feeling _____

_____

_____

A choice I want to make is _____

_____

_____

Any other thoughts? _____

_____

_____

_____

Session 4

Feelings

In this section you will have an opportunity to:

- **Consider feelings as human energy and a gift from God.**

- **Look at the ways in which you identify and deal with feelings.**

- **Understand that throughout life we continue
to learn and relearn new ways to express our feelings.**

All things work to the good of those who love the Lord.
— Romans 8:28

Prayer Reflection

As you continue through this section, you might want to think about these words:

> God, grant me the serenity
> to accept the things I cannot change...
> Courage to change the things I can...
> And, the wisdom to know the difference. — Serenity Prayer

Let's begin by looking at some of your feelings. By naming your feelings and writing them down on paper, you have an opportunity to look at them with the respect they deserve. Feelings are a powerful gift from God—energy that can be used for personal growth and development. Although we may consider some feelings to be "positive" or pleasant and others to be "negative" or unpleasant, feelings are not in themselves morally "good" or "bad." They just "are."

I felt happy or joyful recently when_____

_____

I felt sad recently when _____

_____

I felt fearful or mad recently when_____

_____

Usually, I am able to express my feelings.   Yes   No

If not, what gets in the way? _____

_____

_____

It's difficult for me to express the feeling of _____

because _____

_____

_____

Taking time to think about and express your feelings in your own way is essential for your mental and spiritual health. There are many ways to get in touch with feelings. In some workshops, participants are asked to "name, claim, and proclaim" their true feelings. When in therapy, a person is encouraged to "feel, reveal, and heal." However you choose to label the process of getting in touch with your feelings and the energy they contain, it's important to remember these points:

- Healing hurt feelings, dealing with difficult feelings, or truly understanding feelings is a process with several steps—and it is a lifetime task.

- Becoming aware of a true feeling means naming it, owning it, understanding what's behind it, and working to accept and deal with it on your own terms.

- Understanding yourself takes time and energy.

Feelings As Energy

Generally speaking, we learn at a very young age how to use or channel the energy that comes from feelings. Children watch how the "big people" do it. Parents and other adults in our environment help establish boundaries or appropriate limits around all kinds of feelings—everything from joy, love, and happiness to fears, sadness, and guilt. How we deal with our feelings is learned behavior. Those around us taught us to the best of their abilities what they considered appropriate and inappropriate ways to express feelings.

A parent of one preschooler told this story about his daughter who was excited to be playing with Dad before dinner one evening. Soon it was time for dinner, and he instructed her to pick up the toys and wash up for dinner. The youngster wasn't too excited about cleaning up. Her emphatic, "No, I don't feel like it," was met with an equally emphatic, "I don't care what you're feeling. Wash those hands. Get the germs off. Then sit down at the table." Once at the table, Mom asked everyone to pray before the meal. The girl's prayer took the form of an announcement: "I've had it with this talk of Jesus, germs, and feelings. I've never seen any of them; but grownups talk about them all the time." Her comments reminded her parents that feelings truly are a powerful force, a force that frequently exhibits itself in how we behave.

This young girl was wise beyond her years. We don't get daily glimpses of Jesus, germs, or feelings; however, we do experience the effects of all of them in our lives. Because of differing childhood experiences and backgrounds, we enter adulthood with varying abilities to deal with feelings. Our choices whether or not to express feelings and the way in which we express them can have either a positive or negative impact on our sense of self-worth.

Feelings are energy from inside us. As we grow, we learn certain ways to recognize the energy that comes from feelings and a variety of ways to express or not express that energy. Because this is a learned behavior, we can choose to stop and take time to look at the process. We can then make a choice to alter the way we perceive and deal with our feelings.

Making Use of the Energy in Feelings

Over the years, a myriad of conferences, workshops, sermons, treatment programs, and counseling sessions have been aimed at helping adults—parents and mental health professionals alike—to better understand this God-given human energy and the influence feelings have upon a person's behavior. Diagram 3 is a simplified but valuable chart showing some possible effects of expressing or not expressing certain feelings.

Think of a time when you had a feeling of love or concern for some-one and shared that feeling.

What was the result of that expression of energy? _____

_____

_____

_____

Think of a time when you had a feeling of love or concern for some-one and you did not express that feeling.

What was the result? What got in your way? _____

_____

_____

_____

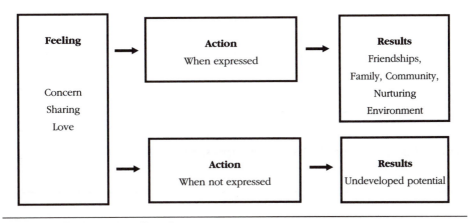

Diagram 3: Feelings Flow Chart I

Having looked at feelings that people commonly consider positive, we will now turn our attention to some feelings viewed by many as "negative." Actually, each is a healthy, normal feeling. It's how we act upon the feeling that creates a positive or negative result. Diagram 4 shows some of the feelings that are more difficult to express.

> Think of a time when you felt hurt or rejected as a result of an encounter with another person. You decided you would risk sharing your feelings with that person.

What happened when you shared your feelings? _____

_____

_____

_____

> Think of another time when you felt hurt or rejected but did not risk sharing the feeling.

What was the result? _____

_____

_____

_____

What influenced your choice not to express yourself? _____

_____

_____

What happened to those feelings?_____

_____

_____

This kind of step-by-step reflection on how you deal with feelings is important because it enables you to identify the stumbling blocks in the process. Having identified the blocks, you can begin to look at the true feelings behind the blocks.

As adults it's not uncommon for us to hide or repress our true feelings— especially if they're unpleasant or we have not learned the skills needed to express them. However, more often than not, this type of behavior leads to frustration, which may result in anger. When we "claim" our true feelings and take a positive step toward expressing all our feelings, we learn new skills. Remember that expressing or dealing with our feelings doesn't always require that we share or vocalize them. We may think them through to a healthy resolution.

One mom tells this story to illustrate how our ways of dealing with feelings change over time. In this instance, those changes allowed her to help her son cope with fear and loneliness. As a child at sleep-over camp for the first time, she was homesick and called her parents. Although very loving and concerned, her parents expressed their thoughts this way, "Be a big girl. Act your age. You shouldn't feel that way. Now, just try to have

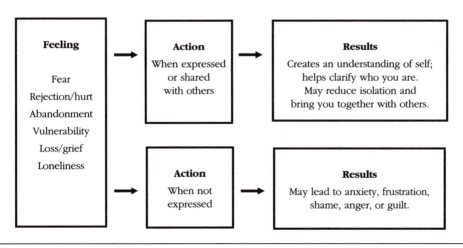

Diagram 4: Feelings Flow Chart II

57

some fun." Throughout her life—as in the lives of many of us—this girl frequently was told by parents and other well-meaning adults how to feel or not feel. Our feelings are personal; while others can try to understand or help us with feelings, no one can help us by dictating how we "should" feel.

That same girl is now a mother and recently was faced with a homesick son at camp. The mother encouraged her son to see that he was having fun at camp but just got a little melancholy when night set in. The mother explained to her son that everyone feels lonely sometimes and that it's OK to feel that way. Mom and Dad missed him, too, but they still were going on about their daily routines and trying to direct that lonely energy into other tasks. This mom had relearned how to express her feelings and help her child learn to express his.

God's Grace Is Present
When We Work Through Our Feelings

The presence of God's breath or spirit (divine energy) within each of us helps create a love for life and for those around us. When evoked, this basic love for life provides the energy we need to maintain deep commitments, to make it through the good times and bad. It comes from deep within the true self, which has the potential to be in balance with all of Creation. This inborn desire for harmony is powerful enough to cause changes within us. These changes work to restore a sense of self-worth when someone or something has violated or hurt us. Energy, when constructively channeled, can lead to changes in our personal lives, in our families, in our communities, and even globally. Gandhi uses these words to express this need to learn to "own" and deal with anger and the energy associated with it:

> I have learned through bitter experience the one supreme lesson
> to conserve my anger, and as heat conserved is transmitted into
> energy, even so our anger controlled can be transmitted into
> power which can move the world.[16]

Take some time to reflect on the idea that conserving anger (for example, not blowing up immediately) can lead to positive changes. Also, remember that when we are able to see anger as a warning light signaling a more primitive feeling of fear, we can take the time to view the energy generated by this fear. We can then hold onto it until we decide how to make a constructive change.

For some of us, childhood experiences of sarcasm, slammed doors, periods of extended silence, "cold wars," and sobbing behind closed doors motivate us to learn to deal directly with our present feelings of hurt, fear of loss, and vulnerability. We understand the pain and confusion associated with the childhood memories and have selected to make a constructive change in our lives. For others, the pattern learned in childhood lives on and leads to anxiety, frustration, anger, and guilt.

To learn to integrate all our feelings, we need to take time to understand what motivates us (clarify values) and make some new choices for our lives. When we realize that it is possible to transform the feeling energy into motivation for change and growth, we are no longer afraid of those choices.

To understand fully how we process our feelings, we need to be aware of the innate desire each of us has to be safely connected to the people and things that are important in our lives. Basic forces deep within each of us move us toward harmony in our relationships. When this connection is really threatened—or when we perceive it is threatened—we experience fear. Because we don't always recognize and deal with the fear, it can manifest itself as anger or frustration.

Time Out — Not Just for Kids

Talk to most parents and educators who use "time out" as a means of discipline and they'll tell you that it works. Adults frequently use "time out" as a means to encourage children to reflect on their behavior and the consequences. It's not surprising that the same process works for adults, too. Reflecting on an emotional situation before reacting is far more productive than arguing, losing your temper, or brooding around in confusion and depression.

Review the following process as one way to deal with situations that lead to anxiety, frustration, and anger.

1. A specific incident happens which threatens a relationship between me and a person or thing I value. I experience a fear of loss, abandonment, or rejection from someone I love.

2. The incident causes some uncomfortable feelings inside me. I need to identify those feelings.

3. My basic reaction is to panic, flee, cry, or explode. In order to make a healthy choice, I need to stop and take time to define clearly: (a) What has happened? (b) What is my reaction? (c) How do I want to respond?

4. It may be helpful to take some deep breaths; take a time out (if the situation is not an emergency); I can slow down my pace so I can think, feel, and decide what my response will be.

5. If I need time and help to clarify my feelings before I can respond, I can consider one of the following options:

- Get away from the cause of the feeling. Find a safe place not connected to the situation or person causing the feeling(s).

- Talk to a trusted friend to express my ideas and better understand my feelings.

- Do something physical—running, chopping wood, cleaning house—to release the excess energy and get in touch with what's happening inside of me.

- Write out the whole experience—the details of what happened and how I feel. Sometimes it's necessary to wait twenty-four hours until you have some distance and a different perspective.

6. Now I can decide what action or communication needs to take place. By taking time to reflect, I can call on the grace that God gives each of us to be in touch with our true selves and to think clearly about what we want (or need) to change. Going to the center of our true self—to a deeper place beyond the initial emotional reaction—allows us to sift, weigh, examine, and choose how we are going to channel our energy honestly and appropriately to bring about change. (Remember that anger always suggests that something or somebody needs to change.)

7. Specify what needs to be changed. Examples: a situation, the way I communicate, my expectations, my limitations, my needs, a behavior.

"My mother was right," said a single parent who read through this process. "She was always telling me to slow down, take a breath, and say a prayer when the going gets rough. I thought she was crazy. What good does it do to pray when you've missed a deadline at work, your kid just lost her tennis shoe, and the dog made a mess on the carpet? I thought it felt better to rant and rave a bit and then forget it. But, after a while, the ranting and raving was out of control. When I slowed down and looked at the big picture, I understood where the feelings were coming from. I started to do something about the cause rather than complaining to everyone around me. Now, instead of screaming, I have a few quiet words with my Maker."

When discussing feelings with groups of women who share the role of motherhood, many say they want to better understand fear, anger, guilt, and shame—where these feelings come from and what to do with them. These feelings, they agree, are a common but poorly understood part of their lives. A thorough understanding of these emotions is important but beyond the scope of this journal. Harriet Goldhor Lerner's *The Dance of Anger* is an excellent reference when working to understand the origin of the angry feelings we all experience from time to time.[17]

Some women also choose to continue their study of feelings with follow-up sessions. Many useful resources are available through church, civic, community, and college groups. The important thing to remember is that new skills to cope with situations in our lives can be learned at any age. As the "Serenity Prayer" reminds us:

> God, grant me the serenity
> to accept the things I cannot change...
> Courage to change the things I can...
> And, the wisdom to know the difference.

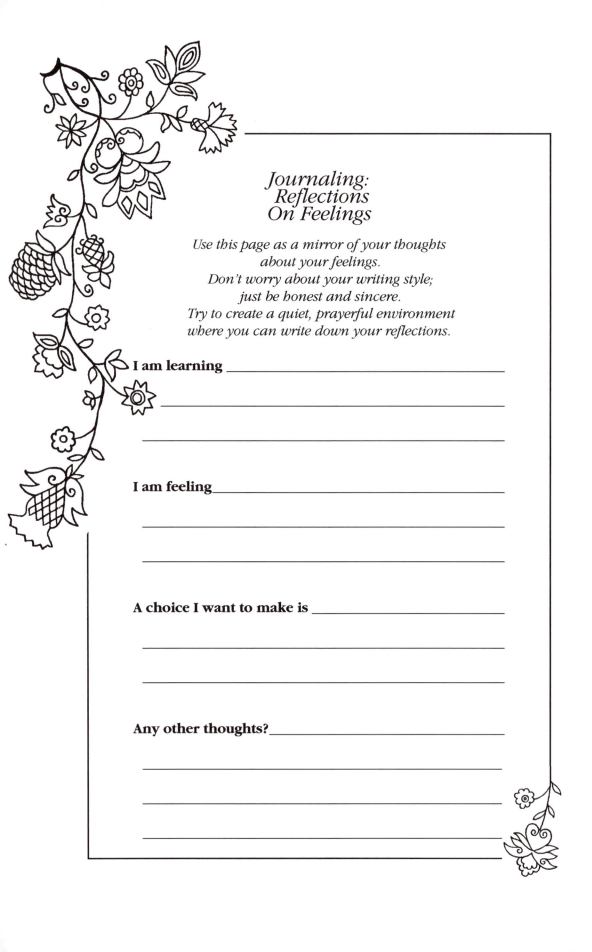

Journaling: Reflections On Feelings

*Use this page as a mirror of your thoughts
about your feelings.
Don't worry about your writing style;
just be honest and sincere.
Try to create a quiet, prayerful environment
where you can write down your reflections.*

I am learning _____

_____

_____

I am feeling_____

_____

_____

A choice I want to make is _____

_____

_____

Any other thoughts?_____

_____

_____

_____

Session 5

Personal Growth

This section is designed to help you:

• **Rediscover the importance of your own mental health needs.**

• **Choose one area where you would like
to improve your overall well-being.**

• **Develop a step-by-step plan that leads
to a change in a behavior or attitude.**

You must put on that new person created in God's image
whose justice and holiness are born of truth.
— Ephesians 4:24

Opening Prayer

Find a quiet place, perhaps light a candle, and make space in your heart to listen to the following words and the images they create for you.

For the Friendship of True Women

Long have I lived and sought to know
The value of things.
To know the gold from the tinsel,
To judge the clowns from the kings.
Love have I known and been glad of,
Joys of the earth have been mine.
But today do I give my thanks
For a rarer gift and find.

For the friendship of true women, Lord,
That has been since the world began.
For the ties of relationships wonderful
That shall hold us as blood bonds may,
For the friendship of true women, Lord,
Take you our thanks today.

Now many the joys I have welcomed
And many the joys that are passed,
But this is one of the blessings unfailing,
And this gives a peace that shall last.
We turn to the arms of our sisters,
We turn for our comforting.
For the friendship of true women, Lord
That has been since the world had breath.

Since a woman stood at a woman's side,
To comfort through birth and death.
That best made us a bond of laughter and tears
That shall last forever and ever.
For the friendship of true women, Lord,
Take you our thanks today.

Now much have I to be glad of,
And much have I sorrowed for,
But nothing is better to hear,
Than the foot of a friend at the door.
And nothing is better to feel
Than the touch of sister's hand,
That says "I know and I understand."

For the friendship of true women, Lord,
That has been and ever shall be,
Since a woman stood at a woman's side
By the cross of Calvary.
For the tears we weep, for the trusts we keep,
For the self-same prayers we pray,
For the friendship of true women, Lord,
Take you my thanks today.[18]

What phrases remind you of a friend? _____

_____

_____

_____

_____

What makes you value this friendship? _____

_____

_____

_____

_____

Making the Choice to Grow in Personal Relationships

Media campaigns and advertising give witness to the deep human desire within all of us for relationships. Subtle advertising ploys try to convince us that using a certain product will win us friends and admirers. Other ads appeal to the emotional side of gift-giving. There's no denying that gifts and cards are appreciated. They can't, however, take the place of time and personal presence that are needed to sustain intimate and true relationships.

Our materialistic, often addictive, society surrounds us with temptations to give all our time, energy, attention, and financial resources to things and experiences that dull our feelings and cloud our interactions with others. We are left with little free time, space, or emotional energy to develop true, lasting friendships. The days of coffee breaks and chats over the backyard fence have been replaced by the push for productivity and more organized activities. Each of us has countless tasks to complete both inside and outside the home. Leisure time is precious and rare for today's average parent. Consider the following story related by one of the women in a MOMS Group:

The Question Was "How (not What) are you doing?"

"How are you doing?" my spiritual advisor asked one day.

"OK," I said, and proceeded to spend ten minutes presenting a litany of all the things I was doing.

This wise, older woman just listened. She didn't interrupt my rambling. She forced me to listen to myself.

By the time I stopped, I realized I was a very busy, very active person; but a person doing too many good things.

She helped me to realize I was doing everything for others and not taking enough time out for myself. "What about soul time? What are you doing to keep yourself alive and well inside?" she asked.

Her gentle questioning led me to realize that I do need and value personal time. I would have to find a way to take some. Personal time is essential for mental and spiritual health.

We are doing ourselves and others an injustice if we fail to take some "soul time" or "quiet time" now and then. Unless we're healthy inside, it's difficult—nearly impossible—to be a good mom, wife, or friend. We need to be a friend to ourselves in order to create true friendships with others. Some of us grew up in very self-sufficient families where little value was placed on friendships. Others looked outside the family for the support and encouragement that was lacking at home. Here again, our experiences shape our perception of friendships and the part they play in our lives.

Following is an exercise designed to help you assess some of the strengths and weaknesses in your attitude toward yourself and others. Once you've gone through each of the eight areas, choose one or more areas in which you would like to change.

Called by God, Fueled by Grace, We Are Ever-Growing, Ever-Changing

Rate yourself as you are thinking and feeling right now. Do this activity with as much honesty as you can. Remember, only you can rate your own attitude and your image of yourself. Circle one number for each item A–H, using the following rating scale:

1 = Describes me most of the time
2 = Fits me quite often—about ¾ of the time
3 = I'm right in the middle—I usually feel either way.

A. I am flexible and open to talking about my needs.

I am rigid, not able to talk about my need.

| 1 | 2 | 3 | 2 | 1 |

B. I accept myself as an individual. I can think my own thoughts and express my thoughts and values in my own way.

I think I must conform to the strongest persons, ideas, and values around me. I have a difficult time accepting my own values, ideas, and choices.

| 1 | 2 | 3 | 2 | 1 |

C. All of my feelings are part of me. I can choose to talk about any of my feelings with a friend.

Only my "good" feelings are acceptable for me to talk about. I choose to keep the rest of my feelings a "secret."

| 1 | 2 | 3 | 2 | 1 |

D. I am able to talk about my most personal feelings with a chosen friend.

I use defenses to protect myself from the pain of talking about my personal feelings with others.

| 1 | 2 | 3 | 2 | 1 |

E. I have energy to give and
   receive affection most of the time.

I often feel too tired to give
or receive affection.

| 1 | 2 | 3 | 2 | 1 |

F. I often feel grateful and relaxed
   and filled with love and joy.

I often feel tense with lots of fear,
anger, and resentments.

| 1 | 2 | 3 | 2 | 1 |

G. I am responsible for my own
   thoughts, feelings, and
   intuitions, and I choose
   my own actions.

Parents or persons in authority
have a lot of control
over my choices
and actions.

| 1 | 2 | 3 | 2 | 1 |

H. I accept myself the way I am
   most of the time.

Most of the time, I am unable
to accept myself as I am.

| 1 | 2 | 3 | 2 | 1 |

Reread the eight items and your responses. If you could "magically" change one of your ratings, which would you choose? Circle that statement.

Rewrite the statement in your own words, saying exactly what you wish you could do.

I wish I could_____

_____

_____

_____

Quietly say this prayer:

> "Dear God, as a woman, trying to fulfill your purpose in giving me life, I ask for the grace to make this change in my attitude or behavior. I pray that I can become a healthier, more fulfilled human being."

These are the steps I want to take to make this happen:

1. _____

_____

2. _____

_____

3. _____

_____

Now take a few minutes of quiet time. Put your body and mind in a state of quiet relaxation. Breathe deeply. Slowly, in your creative imagination, see yourself taking these three steps to accomplish your goal. Try to let your body feel yourself taking the steps with confidence. As you see yourself successfully completing the steps, take a deep breath and feel the benefits of this growth.

When I do this, I feel_____

_____

_____

_____

The exciting part about this activity is that you have the courage and energy to make that magic come true. Seeking God's wisdom and telling a good friend about your desire to change will help reveal just what you need to do to make the change you so deeply desire. These are basic steps toward being a healthier, happier person. We are reminded that the growth process is not static. Rather, it is alive and ever-changing. It provides us with opportunities for new experiences, new insights, and new beginnings.

Reaching Out

I can think of _____,

a friend who helps me to look at my true self and take time for myself.

Call or write this person and tell her how much you value her friendship. If possible, share with her the change you are trying to make. Ask for her support and prayers.

Seeing God's Grace in Personal Growth

The butterfly is a rich, ancient symbol of letting go of life in one form in order to enter into the transformation process and experience new life. As we attempt to let go of old concepts, feelings, intentions, and choices that no longer ring true in our lives, we begin to experience the pain and con-

71

fusion that accompany a transition. Because we have been conditioned to keep peace and avoid pain at any cost, we try to rush our body, mind, and feelings through the pain. This is an impossible task because without that painful death, we are unable to fully experience the resurrection—like the butterfly—to new life.

The Butterfly

Not too fast, not too fast,
Let it grow, let it last,
Nature knows when and why...the butterfly.

I remember one morning when I saw a cocoon in the bark
   of a tree,
I remember I marveled that imprisoned inside was a butterfly
   waiting to be free.

I was very impatient so I warmed the cocoon with the breath
   of my sighs,
And the butterfly trembled and began to emerge like a miracle
   right before my eyes.

All at once I discovered that its delicate wings were all crumpled
   and torn,
When he still wasn't ready I had made him be born.
I was stronger than nature and I had made him be born.

But the wonder of life had a definite plan,
So he died in my hand by the will, not of God, but of man.

Not too fast, not too fast,
Every one has a moment and I'm waiting for mine,
When I'm finally free.
But I mustn't be hurried.
Give me light...give me time.
Like the butterfly...like the butterfly...

Not too fast, not too fast,
Let me grow, let me last.
Nature knows when and why...like the butterfly.[19]

72

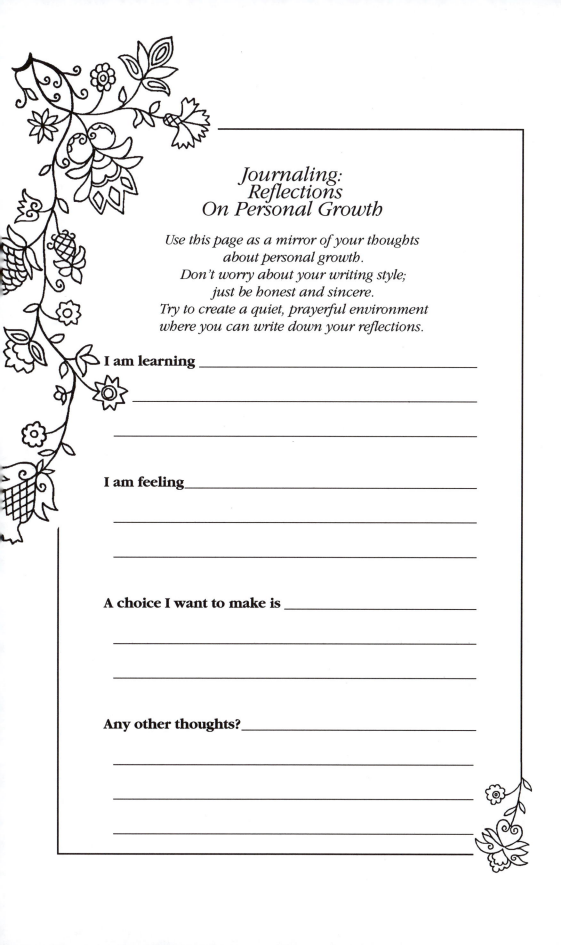

Journaling: Reflections On Personal Growth

*Use this page as a mirror of your thoughts
about personal growth.
Don't worry about your writing style;
just be honest and sincere.
Try to create a quiet, prayerful environment
where you can write down your reflections.*

I am learning _____

_____

_____

I am feeling _____

_____

_____

A choice I want to make is _____

_____

_____

Any other thoughts? _____

_____

_____

_____

More Notes
And Reflections...

Session 6

Expressing Values in Friendships

In this section, you will have a chance to:

- **Look at how you express your values in friendships.**

- **Consider new choices and behaviors to express your values.**

- **Celebrate your values in a new way.**

"There is no greater love than this:
to lay down one's life for one's friends.
You are my friends."
— John 15:13–14

Prayer Reflection

Very early in our lives, a network of persons begins to influence and educate us. Being "connected" to others is obvious as early as toddler play groups. Relationship networks form as soon as we are born and continue as we develop relationships over the years. Let's take a few moments to reflect on God's presence in those relationships, what we have learned from them, and how they have influenced our spiritual growth.

As you pray these words, keep in mind three people who have had a positive influence on your development and ability to express the things you hold near and dear to your heart.

1. _____

2. _____

3. _____

Living God,
loving God,
we thank You
and we praise you
for the power of Your presence
deep in our hearts,
the vitality of Your presence
here in our midst,
for this opportunity
to come together
to affirm our identity
and to celebrate our common hope.
We thank You
for the quality of achievement
that is represented here,
for the many diverse efforts
that continue to contribute
toward the building
　of a better world.
Pour out Your Spirit upon us.
Confirm and strengthen our vision.
Be the Hope that sustains us
and strengthens us
in these changing times.
God of our foremothers
our God forever,
glory and praise!
Amen.[20]

Thank you, God, for _____,

who has affirmed me, influenced me, and helped me express my true

identity.

Choosing and Expressing Values in Relationships

Parenthood in the twentieth century is a challenging profession. Many parents consider it a sacred trust. Parenting entails growth, changes, and the need for continuing education. Although some of this education is rooted in academics, it comes largely from the valuable lessons learned outside the classroom in the school of everyday experience.

Being a parent who is responsible for the health, education, and development of the next generation expands our repertoire of relationships. As we come in contact with new information, new experiences, new feelings, new situations, and new tasks, we cherish relationships with others who are facing the same responsibilities. If we expect our profession as a parent to be the most sacred, challenging, and rewarding aspect of our lives, it will be. It is not a role that exists in isolation. We need the support of other adult friends who share our values.

The responsibility of raising a child is a life-long commitment to the next generation. As child-rearing progresses, our commitment and energy can seem to grow thin. One of the best energy boosts when this happens is to network with other women who share values similar to ours. We learn that we are not alone. We learn that others are experiencing and dealing with challenges just like ours.

Some people believe values are taught. They give little or no credence to the soul or inborn spirit and the part it plays in our value system. Others hold firm to our Christian belief that we are created in the image and likeness of God, while acknowledging the role of experience and learning in the process. Through the centuries, the "source" of these inner values within the person has been hotly discussed, studied, and debated by everyone from the average person on the street to educators and learned philosophers.

As Christians, we believe that with God's first breath of life we are given eternal value. The basic virtues or "soul-values" within each of us reveal themselves in healthy and lasting relationships. These values are the qualities that serve as foundational building blocks for spiritual, emotional, and

77

mental health in each of us. They are qualities such as honesty, respect, and justice. As parents, teachers, and leaders, we show children how to express these internal values through their external behavior.

Each of our lives involves unique past experiences. These experiences include countless interactions with family members and friends and our contacts with the world around us. All of these factors affect the way each individual develops and expresses these basic values. Generally, when both parties in a relationship are able to express their inner values and true selves freely, their relationship blossoms. Friendships can be destroyed when one of the values is neglected or betrayed. Our relationships with friends can also break down when one of us is unaware of priorities in the other's value system.

This lack of awareness can be seen in the example of two women who had on several occasions set times that they would meet for lunch. One friend was always on time or a little early. The other showed up as much as a half-hour late, and on one occasion, called the restaurant with a message to cancel. The "prompt" friend became angry. She valued her carefully planned schedule and feared this behavior was evidence that her friend didn't care about their relationship. The "tardy" friend was disappointed about her delays but took them in stride, not even realizing her behavior was creating confusion for her friend. In this case, some angry words were spoken before the women realized that their differing value priorities—and not their friendship—created the problem.

Values in Friendships

The need for true friendships and the skills needed to maintain those relationships come from within each of us. Included here are basic definitions for fourteen values frequently considered to be among those that form the backbone of healthy adult relationships. As you read them, take a close look at yourself and how you express these values in a specific adult friendship. Note the three values you are able to most freely and fully express in that relationship.

Trust — the ability to be faithful and dependable in my relationships with others

Honesty — the ability to speak the truth, to speak candidly from my perspective

Caring — the ability to act with concern for the needs and feelings of others

Optimism — the ability to view situations and circumstances positively and to communicate a positive attitude

Responsibility — the ability to be accountable for my own behavior and commitments and to respond to others and situations in a reliable manner

Respect — the ability to treat myself and others with reverence and dignity

Sense of humor — the ability to laugh at myself and situations when levity is appropriate

Self-expression — the ability to verbalize my feelings, my needs, my opinions, and my ideas

Affirmation — the ability to recognize and affirm the gifts and strengths of others

Encouragement — the ability to support others constructively, especially in difficult times

Empathy — the ability to relate to the feelings of others

Confidentiality — the ability to keep secrets, to not repeat any personal information shared by others, even when not sworn to secrecy

Acceptance — the ability to accept others whose choices and attitudes differ from my own preferences

Attentiveness — the ability to listen and to spend focused, quality time with another

The three values I can express most freely in that relationship are:

1. _____

2. _____

3. _____

For many of us, this activity can be difficult. We all deeply desire and need friends. We are hurt when a friend fails us or leaves us, or when we realize something just isn't right about a friendship. As we struggle to express our inner self and our values in our external behaviors, we grow spiritually and our relationship skills are developed. Doing this activity helps us look at our true selves, at what we value, and how we can express those values in a specific relationship.

Record here what you learned about yourself through this activity.

I learned _____

_____

_____

Reread the fourteen qualities and select the one or two you are struggling with in a specific relationship.

I wish I could better express the values of _____

_____

_____

As you reflect, ask yourself gently: What gets in the way of my express-ing that value? (For example: Self-expression — I often say what I think the other person wants to hear instead of expressing my real self.)

The attitude or behavior that gets in my way is _____

_____

_____

So that I can better express my values, I would like to _____

_____

_____

For your own growth, you may want to discuss these reflections with a friend or friends. Encourage and support each other on the journey toward self-acceptance and wholeness. Through your discussion, each person will be empowered to continue to develop these God-given values in their lives. A network of women who share their spiritual growth will help you face each day with greater insight and strength. Surround yourself with friends who express values similar to your own.

One MOMS Group took home the above list of values, and each person rewrote her own definition of the fourteen values. The women then listed behaviors that expressed each value. The following week, they compared definitions and discussed the different behaviors for each value. They saw in concrete terms how two people can express the same value in very dif-ferent ways. Conflicts in our friendships are often clarified when we understand what value motivates each person's behavior.

Seeing God's Grace in the Values We Treasure

Each of these fourteen values is a quality we see and feel in the Chris-tian image of God and in the person of Jesus. As we work to better understand our whole self, we see the roots of these virtues deep within our soul. We can see the evolution of these values in our daily behaviors. Sometimes we are attracted to other people because of a specific value(s) we see in them. Almost unconsciously, we try to learn from our relationship with that person how to express that value in ourselves. Actually, all of these values or qualities are interrelated as expressions of the Divine life within each of us. Because we are made in the image and likeness of God, we have a basic or foundational connection to each other.

Miriam Therese Winters' paraphrase of verses from Proverbs calls to mind many of the traits in valiant women through the ages.

> Who shall find a valiant woman?
> Who shall find a woman of strength?
> A pearl of great price is she.
> Her associates all have great confidence
> in her and benefit from her expertise.
> She initiates good, not evil, every day of her life.
> She does not neglect her household tasks,
> she willingly works with her hands.
> Broadminded, her global perspective
> is a source of nurture for her.
> She rises early, before dawn,
> to prepare food for her family
> and organize tasks of the day.
> She considers her options,
> then makes her move,
> investing the experience she already has
> or even profits previously earned.
> She works diligently,
> taking pride in her inner resources and strengths.
> When her gifts are encouraged and her values affirmed,
> she will work well into the night,
> entering wholeheartedly into even the menial tasks.
> She opens her heart to the needy,
> she is generous with the poor,
> yet she does not neglect her family's needs
> nor priorities of her own.
> She is known for her dignity and strength
> and she laughs at the days to come.
> She often speaks with wisdom and she teaches in a kindly way.
> Those who are close to her praise her,
> her family and associates and friends.[21]

Although no one of us can possess all these qualities, these words make it clear that each of us is, in some way, a valiant woman. (Remember, being valiant, virtuous, or good doesn't necessitate striving to be a "Superwoman." It is simply being ourselves to the best of our abilities.) Some of us are especially compassionate and understanding toward friends. Others find domestic chores their strong point. Many labor into the night with sick children or in an effort to complete some important task. Still others have a terrific sense of humor, or wisdom. There are those who have well-developed organizational skills. Take a look at your strengths when you answer these questions.

In what ways am I already a valiant woman? I am _____

_____

_____

I am willing to share my inner resources and strengths with _____

_____

_____

I help my friends grow by _____

_____

_____

Think back to our early discussions about the God-given energy that each of us shares and how this energy is integrated in our thoughts, feelings, and the choices we make. Each of these factors, in turn, affects the relationships in our lives. Because we live in such a mobile, fast-paced, materialistic, consumer-oriented society, friendships can be lost because we don't make the time to clearly express our values in friendships. To be a friend, adults need to choose to take time and make commitments.

These comments by theologian Dick Westley remind each of us that we are a unique and integral part of humankind—that through our relationships we are united.

> The dream of God for humankind, was that they live relationally, in peace, solidarity and redemptive intimacy—thus becoming real signs of God's abiding presence. Human beings are born into families, are born of the intimacy between a man and a woman. Everything about our origins and beginnings bespeaks our ultimate connectedness to one another. We receive the gift of life in relation, and we are to live it relationally and in solidarity with all humankind.[22]

It is with these thoughts in mind that we invite you to complete the final journal page. Your arrival at this point in your journal shows that you have taken the time to explore God's presence within yourself and your friendships.

The time spent with this journal has provided you with a chance to tap into the inner wisdom and strength of your true self—the self given to you by God. That spirit can be strengthened—even in stressful situations—if we can take the time to process our feelings, respect and relish friendships, and attempt to express clearly the things we value.

You now know that new choices are possible. You can now ask yourself: What is my heart's desire? Perhaps the answer is to develop a part of yourself discovered in this journal. Maybe the answer is to reflect on the path your life is taking or to review some old behavior patterns. The choice may be to develop new friendships, nurture longstanding relationships, or to move on to new areas of personal development.

Before making that choice, take time just for you—celebrate the new beginnings this journal has inspired. Treat yourself to something special, something you enjoy. Have lunch with friends. Enjoy some quiet time or prayers with special music. Buy a new plant or fresh flowers. Share your stories with someone special. Then make the choice that will make a difference in your life.

Remember to continue your journey by reading the Postscript and by taking a look some helpful resources for personal growth included in the back of your journal.

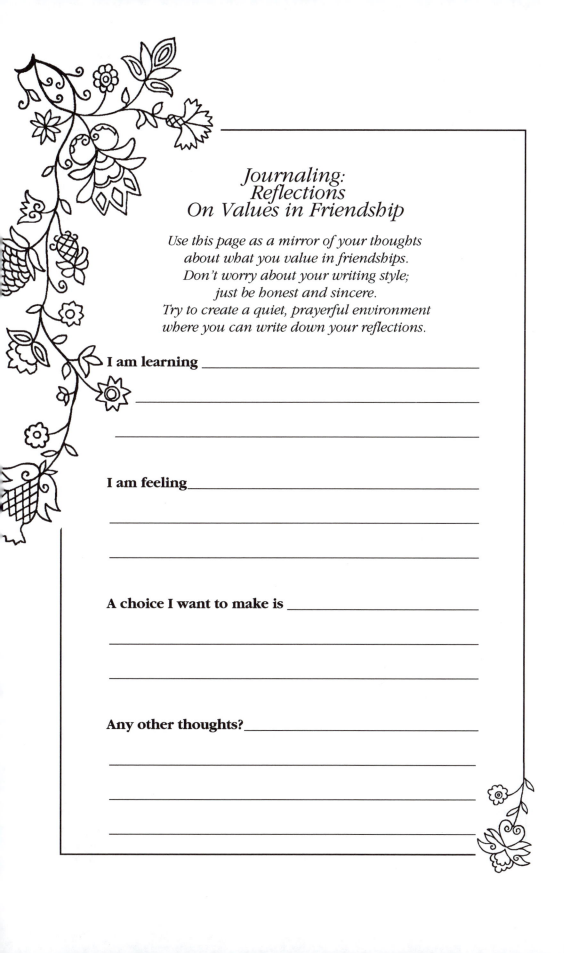

Journaling:
Reflections
On Values in Friendship

*Use this page as a mirror of your thoughts
about what you value in friendships.
Don't worry about your writing style;
just be honest and sincere.
Try to create a quiet, prayerful environment
where you can write down your reflections.*

I am learning _____

_____

_____

I am feeling _____

_____

_____

A choice I want to make is _____

_____

_____

Any other thoughts? _____

_____

_____

_____

*More Notes
And Reflections*

Postscript: Beyond Session 6

Discernment:

Continuing the Journey

In this section, you will have a chance to:

- **Consider the many facets of your life and determine areas in which you are most in need of growth.**

- **Choose whether or not to continue your journey of awareness and spiritual renewal.**

- **Decide how you will maintain or create a healthy balance of in-home and away-from-home activities.**

I know the plans I have in mind for you, plans for your good, not for harm,
offering a future full of hope for you.
— Jeremiah 29:11

What we call the beginning is often the end. And to make an end
is to make a beginning. The end is where we start from.[23]

You have reached the end of your journal and have a new knowledge
of your inner self. The time you spent with this process represents an
opportunity to become more aware of the God-given spirit that enlivens
your being.

This heightened awareness manifests itself in different ways for different
people. For some, it raises to a conscious level feelings of deep gratitude
for the sacredness of their own unique path to wholeness. Many are tear-
fully thankful for the God-given wisdom and strength to progress through
their journey. For others, reflection leads to pain and sadness about
brokenness of spirit or relationships.

As Christians, we believe that the resurrection of Jesus Christ invites
each of us to choose how we participate in a redemptive process. We can
be restored to the fullness of life that God intends for each of us. We need
only seek the grace that leads us to inner peace. That grace is experienced
in many forms, including through prayer, in friendships, with a spiritual
guide, or with the help of a therapist. Each can play a part in the healing
and/or growth process.

Having experienced this new awareness and deeper spiritual renewal,
each person is faced with a decision: What next? Should I seek out ways
to continue the journey? Did I grow? Do I want to continue the growth
process? What really happened to me during this reflective time, during
prayer time, during the sharing of my journal writings with other women?

Here are some choices made by women who completed this journal
alone or in the MOMS group process.

- Continue the spiritual awakening by taking more time alone for
  journaling, private prayer, and reflection.

- Join a spiritual support group consisting of others they can trust or
  with whom they want to build a trusting relationship. The groups
  focused on a variety of topics ranging from women's spirituality to
  marriage enrichment to adult children of alcoholics.

- Take a class, seminar, or workshop on any of the topics of interest
  presented in the journal. Some signed up for study groups in their
  parish, college, or community.

- Face the pain and brokenness by consulting a trained professional. They looked at everything from unresolved childhood/adolescent experiences to marriage issues.

- Attend a parenting class to improve knowledge and skills needed to have better self-esteem as a parent.

- Seek a spiritual guide or director trained in helping persons listen to their inner call to wholeness.

- Look into a journaling workshop to enhance skills in writing down feelings.

- Start a MOMS group in a local congregation as an eight-week experience or as an ongoing ministry. Already in a number of churches, MOMS is an integral part of the faith community. With the support of a pastor or other church leader, lay leaders have relied on materials in *MOMS: Developing a Ministry* [24] to establish the structure, train leaders, and supervise the process.

Women completing the eight weeks frequently report on their evaluations a renewed desire and commitment to make some choice for themselves. Each person has been encouraged to take time to look at and respect her own God-given desires, needs, and gifts. In the process, many find it helpful to share their thoughts with husband, friends, spiritual director, therapist, or clergy person.

As you ponder continuing your journey, we ask you prayerfully to consider the many facets of your life and to determine areas in which you are most in need of growth.

For personal development (physical and/or intellectual), I choose to

_____

_____

_____

In my interpersonal relationships, I choose to pay particular attention to

_____

_____

_____

To maintain or create a healthy balance of in-home and away-from-home activities, I will concentrate on _____

_____

_____

To enrich my innermost self, I choose to _____

_____

_____

A Personal Note As You Close Your Journal And Continue Your Journey

As role models for others, we all hear the advice: "You've got to walk that walk" when teaching or setting examples. We want you to know that we have walked this journey with you. We've shared your grief and frustration, your joy and laughter. The bond of motherhood is what joins us and helps each of us understand how much we need one another. We, too, are continuing our journeys and have found the resources listed on the next pages to be invaluable tools in the process. We also pray that you more deeply come to know God, in whose image we were created, and Jesus, who lived, died, and rose that we might enjoy eternal life.

Paula & Vickie

Resources for the Journey

Included here are just some of the resources to which you may want to turn for more information on topics presented in this book. There are other tremendous resources—in both published and program form—available through bookstores, libraries, adult education programs, church congregations, colleges, and women's groups. Because the area of human growth and the spiritual journey is broader than the confines of a particular denomination or group, we encourage you to branch out in your quest for more information. Resources are grouped in the same order as topics in your journal. Although only listed once for space reasons, a number of publications apply to more than one area of interest.

Session 1: Self-Esteem and Self-Acceptance

Celebrate Yourself: Enhancing Your Own Self-Esteem by Dorothy Corkille Briggs, Doubleday and Company, 1977.

Circle of Stones: Woman's Journey to Herself by Judith Duerk, Luva Media, 1989.

Fritz Kunkel: Selected Writings edited by John A. Stanford, Paulist Press, 1984.

Heal Your Self-Esteem: Recovery From Addictive Thinking by Bryan Robinson, Health Communications, 1991.

Images of Myself by Jean Gill, Paulist Press, 1982.

Learning to Love Yourself: Finding Your Self-Worth by Sharon Wegscheider-Cruse, Health Communications, 1987.

Loving the Christ in You: Spiritual Path to Self- Esteem by George A. Maloney and Barbara J. Rogers-Gardner, Meyer Stone, 1987.

People Making and *The New People Making* by Virginia Satir, Science and Behavior Books, 1988.

The Search for the Beloved: Journeys in Sacred Psychology by Jean Houston, Jeremy P. Tarcher Inc., 1987.

Women and Self-Esteem: Understanding and Improving the Way We Think and Feel About Ourselves by Linda Tschirhart Sanford and Mary Ellen Donovan, Penguin, 1985.

Session 2: Stress, Worries, and Anxiety

Bonkers (Why Women Get Stressed Out and What They Can Do About It) by Kevin Leman, Fleming H. Revell Co., 1987.

Five Minutes' Peace by Kill Murphy, G. P. Putnam's Sons, 1989.

Happiness is an Inside Job by John Powell, SJ, Tabor Publications, 1989.

Happy are You Who Affirm by Thomas A. Kane, Affirmation Books, 1980.

Relax, Recover by Patricia Wuertzer and Lucinda May, Hazelden, 1988.

Religions, Values and Peak Experiences by Abraham Maslow, Viking, 1964-70.

Self-Esteem: A Family Affair by J. I. Clark, Winston Press, 1982.

Real Power: Stages of Personal Power in Organizations by Janet O. Hagberg, Harper/Collins, 1984.

Stress and the Healthy Family by Dolores Curran, Winston Press, 1985.

Transitions: Making Sense of Life's Changes by William Bridges, Addison Wesley, 1980.

Session 3: Everyday Spirituality

Addiction and Grace by Gerald May, Harper and Row, 1988.

Dance of the Spirit: The Seven Steps of Woman's Spirituality by Maria Harris, Bantam Books, 1991.

Growing a Healthy Home edited by Mike Yorkey, Wolgemuth & Hyatt, Publishers, Inc., 1990.

Homecoming: Reclaiming and Championing Your Inner- Child by John Bradshaw, Bantam Books, 1990.

Open Mind, Open Heart by Thomas Keating, Amith House, 1986.

Practical Spirituality for Lay People by Delores Leckey, Sheed and Ward, 1987.

Psalms of a Laywoman by Edwina Gately, Source Books, 1988.

Reclaiming the Connection: A Contemporary Spirituality by Kathleen Fischer, Sheed and Ward, 1990.

Sacred Dwelling: A Spirituality of Family Life by Wendy Wright, Crossroad, 1989.

The Spiritual Life of Children by Robert Coles, Houghton Mifflin Company, 1990.

Wellness Spirituality by John J. Pilch, Crossroad, 1985.

Woman's Spirituality: Resources for Christian Development edited by Joann Wolski Conn, Paulist Press, 1986.

Woman: Her Intuition For Otherness by Eileen P. O'Hea, CSJ, Benedictine Press, 1990.

Session 4: Feelings

Caring Enough to Confront (How to Understand and Express Your Deepest Feelings Toward Others) by David Augsburger, Regal Books, 1973.

Caring, Feeling, Touching by Sidney Simon, Argus Communications, 1976.

Feeling and Healing Your Emotions by Conrad W. Baars, M.D., Logos International, 1979.

Growing Strong in Broken Places by Paula Ripple, Ave Maria Press, 1986.

Hearts That We Broke Long Ago by Muriel Schain, Bantam, 1983.

Prayer That Heals Our Emotions by Eddie Ensley, Contemplative Books 1986.

The Assertive Woman by Stanlee Phelps, MSW, and Nancy Austin, MBA, Impact Publications, 1975.

The Dance of Anger (A Woman's Guide to Changing Patterns) by Harriet Goldhor Lerner, Ph.D, Harper and Row, 1985.

The Gift of Feelings by Paul Tournier, translated by Edwin Hudson, John Knox Press, 1981.

Session 5: Personal Growth

In A Different Voice by Carol Gilligan, Harvard University Press, 1982.

Internal Affairs: A Journal-Keeping Workbook for Self- Intimacy by Kay Leigh Hagan, Harper and Row, 1990.

Making Peace with Your Parents by Harold H. Bloomfield, M.D., and Leonard Felder, Ph.D, Ballantine Books, 1983.

Making Peace with Yourself by Harold H. Bloomfield, M.D., and Leonard Felder, Ph.D, Ballantine Books, 1985.

Merton's Palace of Nowhere: A Search for God Through Awareness of the True Self by Finley James, Ave Maria, 1988.

Pathfinders by Gail Sheehy, William Morrow and Co., 1981.

The Road Less Traveled by M. S. Peck, Simon and Schuster, 1978.

The Star In My Heart: Experiencing Sophia Inner Wisdom by Joyce Rupp, Lura Media, 1990.

Woman's Reality by Anne Wilson Schaef, Winston Press, 1981.

Your Inner Child of the Past by W. Hugh Missildine, Pocket Books, 1983.

Session 6: Expressing Values in Friendship

Breaking Through by Marie Morgan, Winston Press, 1983.

Choice-Making by Sharon Wegscheider-Cruse, Health Communications Inc., 1985.

Connecting with Self and Others by Sherod Miller, Daniel Wackman, Elam Nunnally, and Phyllis Miller, Interpersonal Communication Program Inc., 1988.

Is It Love or Is It Addiction? by Brenda Schaeffer, Harper/Hazeldon, 1987.

Mentoring: The Ministry of Spiritual Kinship by Edward C. Sellner, Ave Maria Press, 1990.

Soul Friend: A Study of Spirituality by Kenneth Leech, Sheldon Press, 1977.

To Dance With God (Family Ritual and Community Celebration) by Gertrude Mueller Nelson, Paulist Press, 1986.

Woman's Ways of Knowing: The Development of Self, Voice and Mind by Mary Field Belenky, Blythe McVicker Clinchy, Nancy Rule Goldberger, and Jill Mattuck Tarule, Basic Books, 1986.

WomanChrist by Christin Lore Weber, Harper and Row, 1987.

Postscript: Discernment: Continuing the Journey

The Dance of Intimacy by H. G. Lerner, Harper & Row Publishers, 1989.

Fighting for Your Marriage: Positive Steps for Preventing Divorce and Preserving a Lasting Love by H. Markman, S. Stanley, and S. L. Blumberg, Jossey-Bass Publishers, 1994.

The Heart of Commitment by S. Stanley, Thomas Nelson Publishers, 1998.

Marriage and the Spirituality of Intimacy by L. Kehrwald, St. Anthony Messenger Press, 1996.

Passionate Marriage by David Schnarch, W. W. Norton & Co., 1997.

The Seven Principles for Making Marriage Work by J. Gottman, Crown Publishers, 1999.

Sixteen Ways to Love Your Lover: Understanding the Sixteen Personality Types So You Can Create a Love That Lasts Forever by O. Kroeger and J. M. Thuesen, Delacorte Press, 1994.

Endnotes

Permission was granted to reprint excerpts from the following sources, copyrighted as noted:

1. Quote attributed to St. Francis de Sales, a bishop and confessor of the 1500s and 1600s, known especially for his meekness. Unable to locate published source.

2. Edwina Gately, *Psalms of a Laywoman* (Trabue Canyon, Calif.: Source Books, 1988), 68.

3. T. S. Eliot, *The Four Quartets* (New York: Harcourt Brace Jovanovich, 1971), 59.

4. *Webster's New World Dictionary*, 3rd ed. (Cleveland: Simon and Schuster, 1988), 584 #11d.

5. Anne E. Carr, *Transforming Grace* (New York: Harper and Row Inc., 1988), 8.

6. *Scripture Readings: Ordinary Time* (Indianapolis: Carmelites, 1990), 277.

7. Sylvester, Sandra M., Ph.D., *Living With Stress.* Carthage, Ill.: Good Apple, 1991), 1–4.

8. Dolores Curran, *Stress and the Healthy Family* (New York: Harper/Collins, 1985).

9. Edward J. Farrell, *Gathering the Fragments* (Detroit: Sacred Heart Seminary, 1987), 22.

10. St. Paul's Letters, *The Catholic Living Bible* (Wheaton, Ill.: Tyndale Publishers, 1971), 130–190.

11. Lisa Laliberte, MOMS Group Leader.

12. Kathleen Hughes, *Lay Presiding: The Art of Leading Prayer* (Collegeville, Minn.: The Liturgical Press, 1990), 35.

13. Maria Harris, *Women and Teaching* (Mahwah, N.J.: Paulist Press, 1988), 12.

14. *The Catholic Living Bible* (Wheaton, Ill.: Tyndale Publishers, 1971), 217.

15. *The Jerusalem Bible* (New York: Doubleday and Delacorte Press, 1966), 231.

16. Gandhi, *Peacemaking: Day by Day* 1 (Erie, Pa.: Pax Christi USA National Catholic Peace Movement, 1989), 24.

17. Harriet Goldhor Lerner, *The Dance of Anger* (New York: Harper and Row Inc., 1985).

18. Theodosia Garrison, *For the Friendship of True Women*. Unable to locate in published sources. Adapted by Paula Hagen, OSB.

19. Sister Therese Even, SSND, *Creative Christian Living* (Fridley, Minn.: Sister Therese Even), 22.

20. Miriam Therese Winter, *Woman Prayer: Woman Song* (New York: Crossroad Continuum, 1987), 116.

21. Ibid, 118.

22. Dick Westley, *A Theology of Presence* (Mystic, Conn.: Twenty-Third Publication, 1989), 61.

23. T. S. Eliot, *Four Quartets* (New York: Harcourt Brace Jovanovich, 1971), 58.

24. Paula Hagen, OSB, and Patricia Hoyt, *MOMS: Developing a Ministry*, rev. ed. (San Jose: Resource Publications, Inc., 1996). This guide details the process of establishing a MOMS group.

More Resources for MOMS

MOMStories
Instant Inspirations for Mothers

Vickie LoPiccolo Jennett, Reflection Questions by Paula Hagen

ISBN 0-89390-445-7, 80 pages, 5.5" x 8.5"

Here are simple, practical, upbeat stories from everyday life that will help young mothers develop their spirituality. This book embodies the point of the MOMS ministry — sharing. Whether dealing with the everyday stresses that leave you feeling frazzled or the unexpected blessings that fill your life with delight, you need to share your stories. *MOMStories*, with space for reflection notes and discussion questions at the end of each story, gently helps the process of sharing. A lectionary index is included for those wishing to tie the stories into the lectionary readings.

MOMStories
Minute Meditations for Mothers

Vickie LoPiccolo Jennett, Reflection Questions by Paula Hagen

ISBN 0-89390-474-0, 80 pages, 5.5" x 8.5"

Inspirational stories help mothers of all ages find meaning in their everyday lives. This book follows up on Vickie Jennett's earlier best-selling work, *MOMStories: Instant Inspiration for Mothers* (see above), and promises to be just as poplular. Mothers read these stories for their own reflection or as the basis for personal sharing within a MOMS group, a faith-sharing ministry that has become a fixture in many churches. *MOMStories: Minute Meditations for Mothers* includes reflection questions at the end of each story, space for notes, instructions for using the book in groups, a thematic index, and an index linking the stories to the lectionary (Cycle B).

For Single Moms

HOW TO FIND MR. OR MS. RIGHT
A Practical Guide to Finding a Soul Mate

Beverly Rodgers and Tom Rodgers

160 pages, 6" x 9", 0-89390-451-1

According to the US Census Bureau the number of singles has more than doubled in the last 25 years. These 44 million singles are left wondering: Why do some people find a lifelong relationship while others stumble from person to person? Is finding a soul mate simple destiny, leaving some lucky and others longing? *How to Find Mr. or Ms. Right* provides hope in the form of a guide that merges the practical with the theoretical, while adding a spiritual dimension that other books lack. The book includes in-depth, yet easy-to-do exercises which foster self-awareness, like finding your "Dreamed about Mate," or the exercise which determines your Imago — your unconscious image of whom you are attracted to. The authors identify several "Love Resisters," like the "Runner or Hider," or the "Clinger or Glomer." The authors show you how these "Love Resisters" can keep you from recognizing your soul mate. And most importantly, the book includes "Your Soul Mate Profile Tool" to help you evaluate prospective partners as objectively as possible, especially when you're in the subjective "in love" state.

"I was 39, single, and very hopeless. I feel that I am married today because I attended a singles workshop and read this book. It taught me what a healthy relationship was all about." — Elizabeth Allen, Human Resource Worker and Workshop Attendee

Beverly and Tom Rodgers founded Rodgers Christian Counseling and work with individuals, couples, and families in the Charlotte, North Carolina, area. Both are members of the American Congress of Christian Counselors and are certified as Imago Therapists by the Institute of Relationship Therapy in New York.

For Couples

SOUL-HEALING LOVE
Ten Practical Easy-to-Learn Techniques for Couples in Crisis

Beverly Rodgers and Thomas A. Rodgers

Paper, 224 pages, 6" x 9", 0-89390-434-1

Is your relationship in trouble? Here is a book that could help get you back on track. Unlike many popular relationship books, this one blends contemporary counseling techniques with biblical principles. The authors aim to help couples overcome the "woundedness in their souls" and achieve the "soul-healing intimacy and oneness" that comes from a deep relationship with God. The ten techniques and exercises found in this book will foster communication, promote empathy, and bring about healing and forgiveness. Try them — and discover God's sacred design for your marriage.

Support for Children

HEARTWAVES
Daily Meditations for Children

Mary S. Burnett

Paper, 192 pages, 5.5" x 8.5", 0-89390-396-5

Children need support. Especially those who are in emotional pain. *Heartwaves* is a daily meditation book, written with simplicity and wit by a school counselor. These 366 stories are based on fact, many of them word for word from children, and are indexed alphabetically by subject. The simple, concrete examples introduce children to such healthy concepts as "setting boundaries" and "detaching" in relationships. Reflections following each story gently suggest a solution to the problem and affirm the child's experience. The author takes a gentle spiritual approach, nudging children toward trusting a higher power operating in their lives. Common themes appearing throughout the book include: respect your feelings, reach out to others, changing what you can. A great tool for support groups. Useful for a broad range of children, from those living with fundamentally healthy families to those living in difficult circumstances. For ages 7-12.

Catechesis in Home and Parish

CELEBRATING THE LECTIONARY CATECHETICAL PACKETS

CELEBRATING THE LECTIONARY (CTL) is a Roman Catholic liturgical catechesis program for parishes, homes and schools. The program offers teacher packets for seven age groups, all coordinated around the same Sunday readings, covering all Sundays from September through May (September through August for the Adult packet). You only need one packet per group because all the handouts are photocopiable, which makes CTL very economical. Additional packets provide for Children's Liturgy of the Word, and bilingual family handout masters, plus support packets for homilists and DREs. Catechize your families using CTL as the core of your catechetical effort. Also use the packets to supplement your at-home education programs and youth ministry. Whatever you do, you don't want to miss the benefits of liturgical catechesis. Call today for details.

FAMILY HANDOUT MASTERS
From Celebrating The Lectionary

Edited by Liz Montes

Looseleaf, 140+ pages, 8½" x 11"
Weekly handouts covering the whole year starting in September

These handouts include a short background on the Sunday and its readings—and they provide several practical and imaginative ways for parents to share their faith, the liturgical year, and Scripture with their children. Use them to involve families in the Sunday readings, or as part of your catechetical program, or for Children's Liturgy of the Word. Photocopy all you need. Bilingual—English and Spanish.

For Reflection

A PRAYER COMPANION FOR MOMS

Vickie Jennett with Paula Hagen

Paper, 104 pages, 4" x 6", 0-89390-265-9

This purse-sized book is for all women who recognize a dimension of the spirituality found in the challenges and joys of motherhood. The authors offer reflections on such everyday experiences as juggling schedules, cleaning the refrigerator, waiting in line, and taking time out for fun. Keep a pen handy, too, because there's space for you to write your own thoughts and feelings.

An excerpt:

Magnificent

The red rocks reaching skyward
      to a blue forever.

The blue forever mingling with
      wisps of white.

The wisps of white bringing
      gentle breezes.

The gentle breezes caressing
      a tear-stained cheek.

The tear-stained cheek turned skyward
      praising God's creation.

Order these books from your local bookseller or call:
1-888-273-7782 (toll free) or 1-408-286-8505
or visit the Resource Publications, Inc., web site at www.rpinet.com